THE

ENGINE

2

COOKBOOK

Books by Rip Esselstyn

The Engine 2 Diet

Plant-Strong

The Engine 2 Seven-Day Rescue Diet

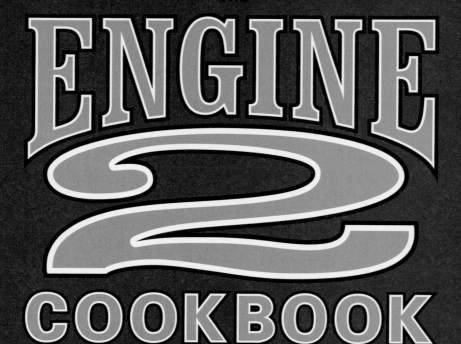

THE ENGINE 2 COOKBOOK

MORE THAN 130 LIP-SMACKING,
RIB-STICKING, BODY-SLIMMING RECIPES
TO LIVE PLANT-STRONG

RIP ESSELSTYN
& JANE ESSELSTYN

GRAND CENTRAL
Life & Style

NEW YORK • BOSTON

The advice herein is not intended to replace the services of trained health professionals, or be a substitute for medical advice. You are advised to consult with your health-care professional with regard to matters relating to your health, and in particular regarding matters that may require diagnosis or medical attention.

Copyright © 2017 by Rip Esselstyn
Photographs copyright © by Donna Turner Ruhlman

Cover design by Danielle Young. Cover copyright © 2017 by Hachette Book Group, Inc.

Hachette Book Group supports the right to free expression and the value of copyright. The purpose of copyright is to encourage writers and artists to produce the creative works that enrich our culture.

The scanning, uploading, and distribution of this book without permission is a theft of the author's intellectual property. If you would like permission to use material from the book (other than for review purposes), please contact permissions@hbgusa.com. Thank you for your support of the author's rights.

Grand Central Life & Style
Hachette Book Group
1290 Avenue of the Americas, New York, NY 10104
grandcentrallifeandstyle.com
twitter.com/grandcentralpub

First Edition: December 2017

Grand Central Life & Style is an imprint of Grand Central Publishing. The Grand Central Life & Style name and logo are trademarks of Hachette Book Group, Inc.

The publisher is not responsible for websites (or their content) that are not owned by the publisher.

The Hachette Speakers Bureau provides a wide range of authors for speaking events. To find out more, go to www.hachettespeakersbureau.com or call (866) 376-6591.

Print book interior design by Danielle Young.

Library of Congress Cataloging-in-Publication Data has been applied for.

ISBNs: 978-1-4555-9120-6 (hardcover); 978-1-4555-9119-0 (ebook)

Printed in the United States of America

QMA

10 9 8 7 6 5 4 3 2 1

To our family:

Essy, Ann,
Rip, Jill, Kole, Sophie, Hope,
Ted, Anne, Flinn, Gus, Rose,
Jane, Brian, Crile, Zeb, Bainon,
Zeb, Polly, Georgie
And any firehouse or friend's house we call our plant-strong home

CONTENTS

I'm an Army Engineer officer stationed at Fort Hood, Texas. After graduating West Point and living the bachelor life of bad food and cheap booze, I struggled to maintain my weight only through rigorous exercise, but it was a constant battle.

Upon returning from my first deployment to Iraq in February 2009, I immediately regained the twenty pounds I had lost during fifteen months of stress and no alcohol... except after several months of crash diets, reduced calorie diets, meal replacement bars, supplements, you name it...I had failed to make any progress. And then I heard Rip being interviewed on the radio. As soon as I got home I looked up the website, ordered his book, read it, decided I was undecided on the "vegan" thing, but I could do anything for four weeks...I took the challenge, all in, 100 percent.

The weight started coming off, sleep got better, my caffeine intake dropped about 80 percent, workouts got better, runs got faster, recovery got shorter...it was incredible; I lost thirteen pounds after four weeks, and about twenty-seven after two-and-a-half months. My cholesterol tested at 127! And I kept the weight off, regardless of fluctuations in my physical activity.

During that summer of 2009 I continued to read and research and became absolutely dedicated to a whole-food, plant-based, vegan lifestyle. I met my now-fiancée, who had been a raw-foodist/vegan for four years, and that common bond was one of several things that brought us together.

I deployed again in February of 2010 to Iraq, and maintained my vegan lifestyle...with some modification as I had to rely heavily on white rice and salad dressings with added sugar, but even with limited food choices, I did it...and that is a testament to how radically my life has changed.

I spend the most amazing time preparing so much incredible, nutritious, delicious raw-vegan food with my fiancée. I feel amazing physically, emotionally, and spiritually.

I spent years in ignorance, spending days off lying on the couch, completely lethargic, addicted to caffeine in order to function, and depressed that I had so little mental and physical energy to do anything but force myself to drag through another week. The Engine 2 diet was the catalyst for not only a life-long personal change, but an ever-growing passion for sharing the gift of optimal health through life-giving plants with others. You have truly blessed me.

Thank you for writing the E2 Diet. Thank you for sharing your story. At the time, as a stereotypical Army officer, I doubt I would have been willing to try a program being touted by a long-haired, tree-hugging, hemp-wearing hippie...but the links of your athletic background and an unspoken bond between military and other public service professions allowed me to be open-minded. So thank you again for being a voice that is reaching an oft-missed demographic.

My life has truly been changed forever, and it started with the E2 Diet.

—BEN JOHNSTON, ARMY ENGINEER OFFICER

My name is Kristen Wade and I am a captain with the Sugar Grove Fire Protection District in the far west suburbs of Chicago. My husband, Al, is a lieutenant with the St. Charles Fire Department. We are both advocates of a plant-based diet and were inspired by your book which we read six years ago and have followed your guidelines ever since. We've additionally "talked" several of our friends—two are sheriff's deputies and another is a paramedic—into shucking off the meat and dairy and embracing the plant-based diet.

My husband and I are both fitness coordinators for our respective departments and compete regularly in marathons and triathlons. We successfully completed our first Ironman on a plant-based diet in 2010 and have since finished two more IMs, nearly 20 marathons and ultra-marathons, and, over the last five years, offroad triathlons including the XTERRA World Championship in Maui, Hawaii, in 2012, 2013, 2015, and 2016. Despite the long training days, meticulous attention to calorie intake, and hours in the gym, we've found great success, lower cholesterol, and higher energy following the E2 plan.

Still I am astounded at how well we've done while eating zero animal protein! I can honestly say I am in the best shape of my life. I even ran a 20-minute 5K during a triathlon. I wasn't able to do this while running cross-country in high school! By the way, I'm thirty-seven. My husband dropped 40 pounds after giving up meat and dairy and can run circles around me...I used to be the fast one...

Again, I would like to thank you for changing the direction of my health and my husband's health and for inspiring us to make a positive and responsible change in the way that we live.

—KRISTEN WADE, FIRE CAPTAIN

PART I

INTRODUCTION

The power and charm of the original Engine 2 story was a bunch of burly, male, Texas firefighters eating a bunch of plants with the courage and chutzpa to just say "no" to all animal products, animal by-products, and processed foods. The reason we were able to do this so successfully and spark a cultural awakening within the Austin Fire Department was because the food resonated with the guys. Plain and simple. This was anything but "turtle food" or "rabbit food." We weren't living on carrot sticks, salad greens, twigs, or berries.

Far from it. We took the four major food groups of the Texas firefighter and plant-strong-ified them! Instead of double cheeseburgers with bacon drenched in mayo with French fries, we feasted on double-decker black bean poblano burgers drenched in salsa and guacamole on whole-grain buns with baked sweet potato fries. Instead of pepperoni pizza with triple cheese, we dined on plant-strong pizza with a triple dose of veggies and fruits including sun-dried tomatoes, pineapples, bell peppers, artichoke hearts, onions, mushrooms, broccoli, and spinach on a whole-grain crust. Instead of beef fajitas sizzling in Crisco we served up portobello mushroom or butternut squash fajitas marinated in red wine with a side of no-fat refried beans with all the fixings. And for dessert, instead of full-fat, cow's udder Blue Bell ice cream, we whipped up frozen bananas, mango, raspberries, or blueberries and made our own fruit sorbets. Real food for real men. The 125 recipes in *The Engine 2 Diet* were reflective of this theme. And for those of you who don't know, one of my favorite sayings is "Real. Men. Eat. Plants!"

The 130-plus recipes in *The Engine 2 Cookbook* go back to the roots of the Engine 2 Diet that resonated with people. If Texas firefighters love to eat this food, your family will as well. It is familiar comfort food with a plant-strong twist: food that sticks to your ribs but not to your arteries. We have assembled easy, hearty, healthy meals so that people and families can rally their kitchens and lifestyles with food that will increase energy levels, decrease weight, improve health, and ease the burden on pocketbooks and the planet.

The strength and impact of the Engine 2 story continues to grow: an Engine 2 plant-strong food line at Whole Foods Market stores; our pinnacle Engine 2 weekend retreat, Plant-Stock, which takes place at the Esselstyn family farm in upstate New York (that has been in the family since 1685); Engine 2 Seven-Day Rescue Immersion programs that take place in Sedona, Arizona, where we show people how to rescue their health with the power of plant-strong food and exercise; and involvement in groundbreaking documentaries like *The Game Changers*. We have also received endless stories of individual empowerment and self-reliance, and of families turning their health around...people saving their own lives. The peer-reviewed scientific studies that have been done over the last thirty years clearly show that all of the major chronic Western diseases—from heart disease to type 2 diabetes, to the major cancers and to obesity—can be slowed down, stopped, or reversed by eating a whole-food, plant-strong diet.

If a bunch of firefighters in the beef capital of the world can learn to eat this way, any house in America can learn to eat this way. I remember what one of my first fire lieutenants used to say: "Firefighters who eat together, fight fires well together." I would echo that any family who cooks together and eats together is engaging in the most powerful yet underutilized tool we have on a daily basis: nurturing our relationships with healthy food. *The Engine 2 Cookbook* is for all those who are looking to take back their health by rallying around these Engine 2 plant-strong recipes that are full of flavor but not full of weak food that can cause your health to suffer.

Plant-Savvy Sister

I want to introduce you to the co-author of this book, my sister, Jane. Jane is two-and-a-half years younger than I am and we have two other brothers, Ted and Zeb. Growing up, the four of us did just about everything together: swam a ton, chopped wood, camped, skied, windsurfed, and also played loads of Monopoly, backgammon, Ping-Pong, and tennis. On Sunday nights our whole family of six would watch *The Six Million Dollar Man* while piled up on our parents' king-size bed. But the one thing we did better than any other family I know was to eat supper together around our lazy Susan table and devour good food and good conversation.

Looking back at our childhood, I realize that eating around that table united our family and allowed us to bond and grow more than any other thing we did together. Although Jane and I were close growing up, we really got the opportunity to connect and grow as adults. In 2011, Jane, a registered nurse, was getting more and more passionate about plant-based nutrition, not only on the educational side, but also in the kitchen—creating one incredible recipe after another. She also developed a knack for explaining major chronic Western diseases in plain language using simple, provocative visual aids, humor, and science—skills she clearly acquired from twenty-plus years of teaching middle-school sex ed. So, who better to ask than Jane to join me at all of our Engine 2 events as a speaker and menu planner to oversee the food? Working together, I discovered what an amazingly upbeat, positive, and creative sister I have, who also has the same level of passion for plant-strong living that I do. I asked her to spearhead the recipe section for my second book, *Plant-Strong,* which came out in 2013, as well as my third book, *The Engine 2 Seven-Day Rescue Diet,* which came out in 2017. When I decided it was time to do a fourth book, a stand-alone *Engine 2 Cookbook,* I knew that Jane was the perfect person to deliver another round of tantalizingly delicious recipes.

CHAPTER 1

FIREFIGHTERS

Everybody loves firefighters. They protect property, save lives, and do just about everything to help people in their communities. Heck, they're modern-day superheroes. They are there for the 4th of July parade to let the kids climb through the fire engine cab, try on the helmets, touch the air packs, and ask an endless stream of crazy questions. They are there to open your car door when it's 98°F after your five-year-old locks himself inside and starts crying hysterically. They are there to put out the fire in your kitchen after you inadvertently left food on the stovetop and went out to run an errand. They are there to rescue your puppy after she falls and gets stuck in the drainage ditch. They are there after your neighbor keels over from a heart attack to start chest compressions and bring her back to life. And they are there to run into burning buildings when everyone else is running out.

Sadly, these superheroes have a higher of death on the job than any other profession. And, surprisingly, firefighters aren't dying in horrific vehicle accidents responding to 911 emergency calls; they aren't dying of smoke inhalation or burns while fighting fires; and they aren't dying when a rooftop or an I beam collapses on them. No, the vast majority of firefighter fatalities are caused by fatal heart attacks.

There are few professions where you are asked to go from 0 to 100 mph in the blink of an eye. Firefighters can be sitting in a chair eating a meal one minute and the next they are throwing on fifty pounds of bunker gear with an air pack, racing through city streets with sirens blaring, pulling 200 feet of hose line from the fire engine, breaking down doors, wielding a charged hose line, and then unleashing its power on the fiery dragon.

Firefighters are constantly pushing their physical limits yet unknowingly overlook the most powerful tool within their grasp to enhance their physical strength and protect them from the grim reaper—food! Instead of fueling their hearts with strong foods that will guard them when the going gets tough, they are burdening their tickers with weak foods that will let them down. This year, over 50 percent of firefighters who die in the line of duty will perish from a disease that is not only preventable but reversible: heart disease. One of the greatest risk factors for heart disease is being overweight or obese. And, according to a study done by *Fire Engineering* magazine, over 83 percent of paid and volunteer firefighters across this country are considered overweight or obese. Amazing! These everyday heroes, the backbone of our communities, have fallen prey to the standard American diet and the foods that are commonly found in their kitchens. It's what's in the kitchens that are killing firefighters.

Kitchens play a key role in the life of a firefighter. In fact, the epicenter of every firehouse is the kitchen—it's the heart and soul and where all the action takes place. It's where the crews converge for meals, huddle up for meetings, and hang out during downtime. It's where crews bond like family. And, believe it or not, it's these same kitchens where everyone breaks bread, laughs, cries, and tells stories. Sadly, many of those stories include tales of firefighter brothers and sisters falling to preventable diseases before their time.

The amount of meat, dairy, and processed food consumed in this country is like an out-of-control freight train. This toxic food environment serves up breakfasts, lunches, and dinners seven days a week, 365 days a year, nonstop. All this food is punishing the hearts, bodies, and brains of the over 1.3 million volunteer and career firefighters across this country. Firefighters, our modern-day supermen and superwomen, are perishing from a modern-day form of kryptonite.

In the Firehouse Kitchen

Let's visit a few different firehouse kitchens to see exactly what I'm talking about:

Your first visit is for breakfast at a fire station in Austin, Texas—my old stomping ground. You walk into the kitchen and there are two firefighters standing over an iconic Viking stove, cooking away. They proudly let you know what they'll be serving the crew of eight this morning: eggs over easy with enough for each firefighter to get two or three, copious amounts of white toast with butter, four pounds of sausage patties, sixteen croissants, and a gallon of whole milk to help slam it all down. Breakfast of Champions?

Your next visit is for lunch at a fire station in Worcester, New Jersey. You stroll into the kitchen and four firefighters have just finished prepping their own lunches. One tailboard firefighter just finished making two ham and cheese sandwiches on white bread with loads of mayo that he'll wash down with a 16-ounce Mountain Dew; the other tailboard firefighter just whipped up Hamburger Helper from the box and is having a side salad of iceberg lettuce drenched with one-fourth of a bottle of ranch dressing; the lieutenant just finished making chicken fajitas with stir-fried onions and bell peppers in canola oil served with cheese and sour cream on white-flour tortillas that he'll polish off with an ice tea sweetened with four packets of sugar. And the driver of the fire engine has ordered a large pepperoni and cheese pizza that she'll devour along with a 20-ounce bottle of Dr. Pepper. For dessert they'll all dive into a gallon of chocolate ice cream. Lunch of Heroes?

Next up for supper is the downtown fire station in Tampa Bay, Florida. You waltz into the kitchen and lo and behold there is more meat than you've seen in one room since your Thanksgiving

SANDBURG BLUE RIDGE CHILI
(page 221)

I am forty-one years old, married, and the father of two. My wife and I have been married for seventeen years and have two awesome boys who are thirteen and ten. I have been in the fire service for twenty-three years and have been with my current department for twenty years where I serve as a captain assigned as the training officer.

In my younger years as a firefighter I always worked out and ate "pretty well," but as the years went by I began, like many of my friends and co-workers, to put on a little extra weight. It wasn't until my late thirties that I noticed the extra weight moved me from the "husky" group to the "chubby" group. I realized that I had used a knee injury and subsequent surgery as an excuse to slow down my workouts. Unfortunately I did not adjust my eating habits and quickly ballooned up to 250 pounds.

I have always served on our department wellness committee and have pushed for annual physicals and structured workouts for years, but now saw myself quickly losing the battle I was trying to support. After a physical last year I had a cholesterol level of 244 and was flirting with a blood pressure that was embarrassingly high.

I knew that the ten-year battle with my weight was not going to be won by just increasing workouts or cutting out the "bad food" of the moment, as pushed by so many "diets of the month."

After another knee surgery (snowboarding this time) I took real stock in my overall health and not just my weight. I also had many people in my life touched by cancer and heart problems. Many of those folks are in the fire service and are younger than I am! I was determined to not expect a different result from the same old actions.

I am a voracious reader and started to look around. Your book, *The Engine 2 Diet,* was one that completely changed my view on food.

On my hire date anniversary I made a complete switch to the plant-strong way of eating. COLD TURKEY! My wife was very skeptical and not just because I make the best BBQ sauce you have ever had. But after only two weeks we saw some amazing results. By week three she was in!

At three months, I had dropped 25 pounds, dropped my blood pressure by 20 points, and am confident that there is a drop in my cholesterol. I feel amazing. I sleep better, I wake up easier, and my energy level is through the roof.

I cannot tell you how great I feel. I feel like I have found out some secret and I need to tell everyone!

—BRIAN HYATT, FIRE CAPTAIN

family reunion five years ago. This is the big daddy of all fire stations. It houses two fire engines, a fire truck, and the battalion chief's vehicle. In sum total there are thirteen firefighters manning the station at all times. The kitchen is a whirl of activity with mounds of food being placed on the kitchen table: a meat loaf the size of Wisconsin, four deep-fried chickens, a honey-baked ham, a trough of macaroni and cheese, a massive bowl of mashed potatoes with pools of butter on top with a side of white gravy, and four pounds of green beans from a can. For dessert, add three apple pies and two gallons of cookies and cream ice cream. And to drink, it's Coca-Cola around the horn! Supper of Superheroes?

Next you decide to make a visit to a fire rescue station in Red Hook, New York. You've heard whispers about a group of firefighters from Brooklyn who have embraced the plant-strong lifestyle but you want to see it with your own eyes. You drop by and find there are five firefighters at the station and three of them are in the kitchen, cooking and preparing an Engine 2–inspired breakfast. What's on the menu?

Sitting on the stove in a large pot is a fresh batch of steel-cut oatmeal. On the counter in six smaller bowls are the toppings that will go on the oatmeal: sliced strawberries, golden raisins, sliced bananas, chia seeds, toasted walnut pieces, and fresh blueberries. And to drink: good old H_2O. Breakfast of Champions!

What are they planning for lunch? They tell you in a few hours they'll be feasting on a batch of monstrous homemade veggie burgers with tomatoes, caramelized onions, pan-seared mushrooms, guacamole, and salsa on a 100 percent whole-grain bun. On the side they'll be having baked sweet potato fries along with steamed broccoli with a walnut dressing. Lunch of Heroes!

How about dinner? After a CrossFit-style workout late in the afternoon, the crew will once again converge on the kitchen for supper. On the menu: black bean and sweet potato quesadillas, roasted cauliflower steaks with a low-sodium tamari/nutritional yeast glaze, and a monstrous salad of spinach, kale, roasted corn, red bell peppers, and roasted Yukon gold potato chunks with a Sweet Fire oil-free dressing. For dessert? Homemade banana ice cream with a sprinkling of toasted oats and a chocolate balsamic glaze on top. And to drink there's ice cold water with a hint of fresh mint and strawberries. Now that sounds like the Supper of Superheroes!

All of the food all day long is plant-strong, and all of it is made without any added oils and with minimal salt and minimal added sugars. And there are never any leftovers!

Unfortunately, this strong style of eating is the exception to the rule. Most fire stations are fixing up meals where meat is king, dairy is queen, and fruits, vegetables, whole grains, and beans have been kicked to the curb as not being manly enough to earn a seat at the firehouse kitchen table. This is the way the world turns in firehouse kitchens.

And it's not only firefighters' kitchens that are serving an alarming amount of unhealthy food. The same is true of most kitchens in America. All of this weak food is causing our collective health to spiral out of control. We are plagued with heart disease, riddled with cancers, and facing a pandemic of diabetes and obesity. Let's call a spade a spade: The standard American diet leads to standard

American diseases and standard American death. The white elephant in the room is that these diseases are manifestations of all the meat, cheese, dairy, and processed foods we are eating. The good news is that all of these diseases can be halted, prevented, or reversed by simply changing the way you eat.

Simultaneously, we have a major planetary crisis occurring: global climate change, what many experts consider to be the single greatest threat facing humanity today. Mother Earth is heating up and she is crying out for help. As a result, we are experiencing record numbers of floods, droughts, and wildfires across the globe. What's more, this rise in global temperatures is causing irreversible changes: ice caps are melting, dead zones are forming in the oceans, previously arable land is turning to desert, and species are being pushed toward extinction. Until recently we thought animal agriculture was responsible for 17 percent of all global greenhouse gas emissions. However, the latest research from the World Bank and Worldwatch Institute place it at a staggering 51 percent, four times that of all transportation emissions (cars, trucks, trains, boats, and planes) combined! And again, this damage to our environment is the manifestation of our food choices and specifically the supply chain and the life cycle of all animal agriculture! The good news is the most effective thing you can do—starting tomorrow—if you truly consider yourself to be a good steward of this planet is to change the food in your kitchen.

Even more good news is that pioneering individuals have been paving the way for us for over thirty years. This is an important number because this is typically how long it takes for the medical establishment and our culture to accept "new" ideas that can help people and save lives.

Case in point, my great-grandfather, George Washington Crile, was a visionary physician, scientist, and pioneering and forward-thinking man. In 1921 he founded the famed Cleveland Clinic. In the late 1890s, he performed the first successful blood transfusion from one human being to another. He figured out the technology and wrote about it extensively in the medical literature and spoke about it everywhere he went. In his autobiography when he wrote about blood transfusions he mentions how unfortunate it was that it took almost thirty years for the medical community to accept this technology. Thousands and thousands of lives could have been saved,

ROASTED CAULIFLOWER STEAKS
(page 129)

especially during World War I. In the last sentence of this chapter he wrote, "But such is the inertia of the human race."

Another example of how human inertia can prevent advancement is the pioneering work of my grandfather, George "Barney" Crile, the son of George Washington Crile. Barney learned a technique when he was in London called the partial mastectomy or lumpectomy for women with breast cancer: Instead of removing the whole breast, the surrounding muscle, and lymph nodes, the only thing that is removed is the tumor itself. Although it was much less disfiguring and had the same long-term results, the medical community in America wanted nothing to do with the procedure. Barney was labeled a traitor and a quack and was blacklisted, but he held tight to his guns and almost thirty years later the partial mastectomy became accepted. It is now one of the more common procedures in medicine.

Another example of the establishment's long delays in accepting new ideas is the Heimlich maneuver. Dr. Henry Heimlich, a thoracic surgeon, came up with the technique in the mid-1950s. He discovered that the amount of air in the thoracic cavity is immense and, by pushing in on the xiphoid process (the lower part of the sternum), one can generate an amazing amount of pressure that can help force out an object lodged in a person's windpipe. When he presented my father with the Benjamin Spock Award for Compassion in Medicine in 2005, he mentioned how as a pioneer you get arrows shot at your back all day long. He also mentioned how it took almost twenty-five years before the American Red Cross and the American Heart Association started endorsing the Heimlich maneuver for choking victims. Up to that point the recommended approach was a blow to the back, which is known to potentially lodge the object even deeper and firmer into the windpipe.

Cigarettes are another subject where it took some time to recognize their damaging effects and make changes to policy. In the 1950s doctors, the government, celebrities, and even Santa Claus— yes, Santa Claus—endorsed cigarettes as being good for your health, sex life, and for increasing energy. It took over 7,000 studies in the medical literature before the medical community stood up and took notice in the mid-1960s of the negative impact of smoking. And today, in 2018, it's a whole new ballgame. We have effectively eradicated the amount of smokers in this country from over 50 percent in the 1950s and 1960s to less than 20 percent today.

More recently, we've seen the establishment's nutritional defiance with the number one killer of men and women in this country: heart disease. We know from my father's and Dr. Dean Ornish's research going back to the early 1980s that none of us need to die of a heart attack or stroke. Both of these bold physicians have unequivocally shown, using before and after angiographic evidence, that the body has the ability to metabolize away the plaque formations in the artery walls by transitioning to a low-fat, whole-food, plant-strong diet. And yet, most physicians and cardiologists don't think that their patients can do something as radical as eat a bunch of plants and would prefer to try and solve this epidemic with pills and procedures, methods that don't address the root cause of the disease. However, there is hope not only in the medical community but also among cardiologists. In 2016, the president of the American College of Cardiology, Dr. Kim Williams, not only endorsed this type of lifestyle for his patients but also started eating this way himself. When asked why he doesn't eat meat he replied: "We know that red meat kills you. And we know that processed meat kills you even faster. I know I'm going to die but I just don't want it to be my fault!" He's also gone so far as to say that there are two types of doctors: those who are following a plant-based diet and those who have yet to read the science.

There's a saying that you can't break a glass bottle from the inside. That's exactly what we're trying to do today with the health-care crisis and the climate change crisis that is afoot. It's time to think outside the glass bottle, to think outside the medical profession, to think beyond more pills and procedures, to think beyond solar power, windmills, and electric cars. It's time to embrace the most basic, economical, effective, and fundamental thing in the world: the food in our kitchens. By doing this you can not only break that glass bottle, you can shatter it to smithereens!

Let's not wait another thirty years, or heck, even another ten years, before we take the kale by the horns and collectively make a change. We are smarter and better than that. Let's be brave and bold and do our part to start a tectonic shift in our habits and relationship with food so we can protect our health and the health of our planet. Let's not look back and ask why...instead let's look ahead and ask why not.

Find the firefighter inside each and every one of you and climb on board the Engine 2 fire engine and join the team. It starts and ends with the food in our kitchens. What's in your kitchen? What foods are stocked in your cupboards? What foods are loaded in your fridge and freezer? Take inventory and put your best plant-strong foot forward!

It is Jane's and my hope that the recipes in this cookbook will inspire you to start eating plant-strong or re-inspire you to continue your plant-strong journey. It's the path that can save all of us, and it starts with you!

I've always been very active and health conscious. Now that I'm older I swim to stay in shape, when I was younger I played a lot of basketball that over the years took its toll on my knees. Recently my doctors informed me that both knees are bone on bone and my right knee had a nasty Popliteal Cyst (Baker's Cyst) making it very painful...I was crawling up the stairs in our home. We scheduled a double knee replacement to be performed in October. I wanted to be in the best possible shape before going under the knife so a friend recommended the *Forks over Knives* and *The Engine 2 Diet* videos. I watched them both and got on the plan in July. In less than 2 months all the inflammation and pain in both knees was gone and the Baker's Cyst dried up. I said to my wife, "If my knees felt this good I never would have gone to see the doctor in the first place." Bottom line, I've cancelled my double knee replacement surgery. In addition to my knees feeling great I lost 10 pounds and my cholesterol dropped from 189 to 159. I love the food, I'm never hungry, and I'm spreading the word. I already have my wife and a few friends on board.

Thanks a million Rip and Stay Plant Strong!

—TOM WEBER, 59, REAL ESTATE PROFESSIONAL

CHAPTER 2

GETTING YOUR KITCHEN IN PLANT-STRONG SHAPE

I am Jane, Rip's younger sister. I am a mom, a nurse, a researcher, a wife, an athlete, a cookbook author, a middle-school sex-ed teacher, and co-captain of my family's plant-strong kitchen. So how do you get your kitchen into plant-strong shape? It's no problem to whip it into shape.

We adopted this way of plant-based eating around 1984. At the time, we were all still living under our parents' roof. This was before the invention of the Internet, so we all listened to whatever our father was fired up about. He read study after study to us all in the living room or at the dinner table and although sometimes we would fall asleep or drift off in no time flat, he successfully drilled the message into all of us—eating a plant-based diet is best for a healthy life. We all absorbed enough of this message to leave our parents' home following our plant-based compasses. It doesn't take much to get your kitchen plant-friendly and your diet heart-healthy.

The Engine 2 Cookbook Guidelines

All our books promote a plant-strong lifestyle, which means we are big advocates of plants and denounce animal products and animal by-products.

FOODS TO AVOID
- Meat
- Dairy
- Added oils

FOODS TO EMBRACE
- Fruits
- Legumes: beans, peas, lentils
- Nuts and seeds
- Vegetables
- Whole grains

INGREDIENTS TO USE SPARINGLY
- Added sweeteners
- Added sodium

Stocking Up

From decades of experience, here are a few of my tips for stocking a plant-based kitchen. Think of your trip to the grocery store like hitting a home run.

First base: produce section—grab a ton of fresh fruit, veggies, greens, potatoes, squash, mushrooms, fresh salsas, and herbs.

Second base: the frozen section—fruits, veggies, and prepared grains.

Third base: the middle of the store for beans, cereals, nondairy milk, grains, the bulk section, flours, salsa, peanut butter, vinegar, ketchup, mustard, and BBQ sauce (keeping in mind *no meat, no dairy, no high-fructose corn syrup, and minimal salt or sweetener added*).

Home: the checkout counter.

That is how I round the bases at my grocery store.

Cooking in the Plant-Strong Kitchen

How much space do you need for a plant-strong kitchen?

After teaching a cooking class out of my home, a participant said, "It is so good to see you can cook healthy food for your family so simply and in such a small space" (gesturing around our kitchen). I had never thought of our kitchen as anything more or less than what I needed. I always comfortably created meals for my family and myself—never wishing for more surface area to cover with bowls, pans, mess, or clutter, and more to clean. Point being, you do not need a big, beautiful, or new kitchen to be plant-strong. Be brave. Be bold. Just start!

What are the essentials for a plant-strong kitchen?
KITCHEN BASICS

You'll need a kitchen sink, a stove, a power source, and ideally an oven or a toaster oven.

IN THE CUPBOARDS AND ON THE COUNTER
- Three pots: one small, one medium, and one large. Two pans: one small and one large skillet, ideally one of them non-stick
- Baking sheet and baking dish
- Cutting board and two knives: a big sharp knife (like the ones in scary movies) and a small serrated knife
- Wooden spoon, rubber spatula, scissors, can opener, two mixing bowls, parchment paper, storage containers
- Plates, bowls, forks, spoons, knives

I found the Engine 2 Seven-Day Rescue Diet after decades of struggling to follow eating plans that were so restrictive I could not maintain them. Even as a vegan I gained weight, eventually reaching 385 pounds. Inevitably, I had diabetes mellitus type 2 and hypertension. I would lose some weight, and gain some weight. After losing 40 pounds in about a year, I still had out of control blood glucose levels despite medications. I started the Seven-Day Rescue carrying 345 pounds, with a glucose reading of over 400mg/dL (it should be less than 130). I thought *there is no way that eating this way can work, but at least it is different and I can eat more.* In the first week, my glucose readings dropped into the normal range and became stable. I am now in my tenth week of living the Seven-Day Rescue. I have lost 38 pounds. I am off all medications. In a month, I will run my first 5k race. I am plant-strong for life.

Trust the plan. Follow it 100 percent. Accept no excuses. Never stop.

—JOSEPH ALEXANDER, MS, MPHIL, RN, ROCHESTER, MINNESOTA

OPTIONAL GADGETS, MACHINES, TIME SAVERS

- Rice cooker, microwave, lemon press (catches the seeds), lemon zester
- Food processor or high-speed blender, immersion blender, sandwich grill (like a panini maker), Instapot pressure cooker, Yonanas frozen dessert maker (or a Dessert Bullet)

What foods are part of the plant-strong kitchen?

The amount of whole, plant-based foods available is endless: Grains, greens, beans, legumes, lentils, veggies, fruits, roots, mushrooms, berries, nuts, seeds, herbs, and spices will fill your fridge and pantry.

What will you grab from the grocery store or farmers' market?

- Bulk items: Check out the variety available and their prices. Often bulk items are a better deal for whole grains, nuts, seeds, spices, and nutritional yeast.
- Canned goods (beans, vegetables—low-sodium, no-fat, vegetarian)
- Dried beans
- Condiments (no high-fructose corn syrup)
- Dried fruit
- Fresh produce
- Frozen fruits, vegetables, prepared grains
- Nuts and seeds
- Spices
- Whole grains, whole-grain breads, corn and flour tortillas with no added oils

What is batch cooking? And how will it help your plant-strong kitchen?

Batch cooking simply means consciously preparing extra food ahead of time. Here are a few ways to do this:

- Passive batch cooking: Prepare loads of the complex carbohydrates and grains you love. These are usually the time-demanding parts of the meal. Make a bucket of oatmeal, a vat of brown rice, a trough of quinoa; or prepare a sack of potatoes, a tray of sweet potatoes, or a load of whichever whole grain you prefer. All of these can be done *passively*—while the game is on, while you are mowing the lawn, while you watch Netflix, or while you are on a run. Store them in your fridge for the week ahead.

- Active batch cooking: Whenever you make a sauce, hummus, spread, salsa, dressings, or dried beans, make extra by doubling, tripling, or quadrupling the recipe. Most recipes last up to five days when stored properly in the fridge. The key is to store some for later in the week. For example: If I see we have Mighty Mango Salsa (page 86) left over, dinner is done. Here is how: Grab a batch-cooked sweet potato, a cup of batch-cooked brown rice, a can of black beans, a few shakes of spice, and a kick of hot sauce and mix it all together. Warm it up between two whole-grain tortillas and top with that batch-cooked Mighty Mango Salsa. Done and delicious! A fridge with any amount of Kale Butter 3.0 (page 58), Beet Butter (page 61), Jalapeño Walnut Sauce and Spread (page 57), or True Grit Gravy (page 79) lets your eyes and stomach know there are good things coming your way soon! Reduce your stress and *actively* batch cook when you can!

I was diagnosed with high cholesterol eleven years ago. My doctor wanted me to go on medication immediately because I am thin and he didn't think diet could help me at all. Nevertheless, I changed my diet and for the past eleven years I have been able to hang between 195 and 215 mg/dl, which was acceptable to me. A couple of months ago, I read an article about the Engine 2 Diet. I checked out the book from the library, read it, and then bought it and decided to give it a go.

One day, as I was driving to have my cholesterol tested, I was thinking what kind of number I would need to make me continue working on this new diet. I was at 212 the last time I was tested. I figured it would have to be at least 192 to get me to keep going with the Engine 2 diet. My cholesterol was 143! I was ecstatic!!! I didn't imagine in my wildest dreams that I would ever see this kind of number.

—DEBBIE CARTER

What will you throw out of your kitchen?
(Yes, we mean in the garbage, and out of the house.)

- Dairy in all forms
- Eggs
- Meat
- All oils or anything with oil in the ingredients
- Sugar
- White flour

Forge ahead with your arsenal of plants. You will feel protected and powerful, clear-eyed and full of energy. Do not let processed foods block your view. As I always say, "Be brave. Be bold. Just start!"

Have a blast creating plant-based food you can serve at every meal, from filling breakfasts to tasty snacks to delicious dinners. We make knockout veggie burgers instead of hamburgers, thick veggie chili instead of greasy meat chili, exploding burritos filled with rice, beans, and veggies (no meat and sour cream), delicious hearty scones, cookies, puddings, parfaits, and soft serve instead of dairy, eggs, and oil-filled sweets. I have to be honest: Not every dish is a hit—ask my three teenagers. But if something isn't a home run, we can try again with variations of plant-strong ingredients—the possibilities are endless.

It is so exciting to discover the next recipe that the plant-based universe and this cookbook wants to reveal! There really is plant-based food out there for everyone. There is no way we could keep up with this way of eating if it was not easy to maintain and did not make us feel great. Every year we eat this way we get better and better at it. It truly is a matter of doing it. Don't be afraid of recipes you see elsewhere that look good to you but are not (yet) plant-strong, as you can always skip the added oil, use nondairy milk, and try spices instead of all the added salt. Be brave. Be bold. Just start!

PART II

LIP-SMACKING, RIB-STICKING, BODY-SLIMMING RECIPES

FOLDED CHICKPEA OMELETS
(page 50)

CHAPTER 3

BREAKFAST

SUNDAY MORNING BLUEBERRY PANCAKES

Our kids always want pancakes on the weekend—as a treat after a long swim practice or simply after waking up late. It has become a tradition we love, especially when it is berry season! Blueberries are one of the few blue foods in the world, and when it comes to berries they are in a class of their own. Their blue color is an indicator of the insane amount of antioxidants they contain.

Makes 8 to 10 (3-inch) pancakes

1 cup white whole wheat flour (we prefer King Arthur brand)

1 cup oat flour

1 tablespoon baking powder

2 tablespoons flaxseed meal

¼ teaspoon salt

1¾ cups oat milk or almond milk

1 tablespoon 100% pure maple syrup

1½ teaspoons vanilla extract

1 cup (or however much you want) blueberries, or raspberries, or banana slices if you prefer, or Quick Blueberry Topping (page 103)

In a bowl, combine the whole wheat flour, oat flour, baking powder, flaxseed meal, and salt. In another bowl, combine the milk, maple syrup, and vanilla and stir. Add the dry ingredients to the wet ingredients and stir until incorporated.

In a nonstick skillet over medium heat, ladle batter into the pan. Drop blueberries (or raspberries or banana slices) to the raw side of the pancake as soon as you can, otherwise the raw batter cooks too much to hold the blueberries. Cook until the batter begins to bubble and the bottom of the pancake is golden (use the edge of the spatula to peek under the pancake). Flip and cook on the other side until golden. Repeat with the remaining batter.

Top the pancakes with more blueberries, raspberries, banana slices, some blueberry topping, or a kiss of pure maple syrup.

SEDONA SWEET POTATO WAFFLES

These incredible sweet potato waffles were the brilliant creation of Engine 2's traveling chef, Brenda Reed. One morning she found herself in a not-enough-waffle-batter kitchen crisis while managing the crew at one of our Engine 2 week-long immersion events in beautiful Sedona, Arizona. Using leftover sweet potatoes and her plant-strong intuition, she whipped up these waffles and everyone swooned over them!

BRENDA'S TIP: "These are a great way to use extra sweet potatoes!"

Makes 6 waffles

2 tablespoons flaxseed meal

¼ cup water

1½ cups oat flour

1 teaspoon baking powder

½ teaspoon baking soda

2 teaspoons cinnamon

1½ cups oat milk

1 teaspoon apple cider vinegar

1 teaspoon vanilla extract

1 to 2 tablespoons 100% pure maple syrup

⅓ cup smashed cooked peeled sweet potato

Quick Blueberry Topping (page 103), maple syrup, strawberries, or fresh fruit, for serving

Preheat a nonstick waffle maker.

In a small bowl, combine the flaxseed meal and water. Set aside.

In a mixing bowl, combine the oat flour, baking powder, baking soda, and cinnamon and gently stir together. Add the oat milk, vinegar, vanilla, maple syrup (to taste), and sweet potato. Mix together well—some sweet potato pieces are fun to bite into, but not too many.

Pour batter into each section of your waffle maker, close the lid and bake as directed.

Drizzle with blueberry topping or a wee bit of maple syrup, or top with fresh fruit.

BIG HIT WAFFLES

Our youngest brother, Zeb, has a daughter named Georgie. When she was four years old she asked him to make these waffles for her school's Share Day. The preschool kids devoured the oats, flaxseed meal, lemon, and banana filled waffles! Soon all the preschool parents were hitting up Zeb for the recipe!

Makes 6 waffles

2 cups almond milk

1 cup unsweetened applesauce

2 cups old-fashioned oats

½ teaspoon baking soda

½ cup walnuts, in pieces

1 medium banana, smashed

¼ cup flaxseed meal

Grated zest of 1 lemon

1 teaspoon cinnamon

¼ teaspoon vanilla extract

Fresh fruit, 100% maple syrup, or Quick Blueberry Topping (page 103), for serving (optional)

Preheat a nonstick waffle maker.

In a food processor or high-speed blender, combine the milk, applesauce, oats, baking soda, walnuts, banana, flaxseed meal, lemon zest, cinnamon, and vanilla until they form a thick batter.

Pour batter into each section of your waffle maker, close the lid and bake as directed. Gently remove the waffle when done.

Repeat with the remaining batter to make 6 waffles. Freeze leftovers for a quick breakfast or snack.

The waffles are good plain, or top them with fruit and a drizzle of syrup or berry topping.

SEED BARK GRANOLA

This recipe is the answer to many questions: What to add on top of oatmeal? What to eat instead of oatmeal? What to use for a crispy crust? What to take on hiking trips or road trips? What to give as a teacher gift? What to use in the Raspberry Pudding Crumble Parfait (page 253)? What to bring as a party favor? What to make for a nut-free, gluten-free bake sale (see Seed Bark Pucks page 248)? Read on and see why this recipe is the answer!

Make 3-plus cups granola (depending on size of clumps)

1½ cups raw pumpkin seeds

½ cup raw sunflower seeds

¼ cup raw sesame seeds

¼ cup flaxseed meal

2 tablespoons chia seeds

2 to 3 tablespoons 100% pure maple syrup (just enough to barely coat the blended ingredients)

Preheat the oven to 350°F. Line a baking sheet with parchment paper.

In a bowl, combine the pumpkin seeds, sunflower seeds, sesame seeds, flaxseed meal, chia seeds, and maple syrup. Toss all the ingredients until well coated. Place the mixture onto the lined pan and press out to about ¼- to ⅓-inch thickness.

Bake for 18 minutes, until fragrant and lightly browned on top. Rotate the pan halfway through if your oven bakes unevenly. Do not let the granola burn.

Remove from the oven and let cool; you can hear the granola crackling as it cools. This is an important stage as this is when it stiffens and gets crispy. After cooling for 20 minutes, pick up the baking sheet a few inches in the air and let it fall onto the counter. This helps the granola shatter into pieces—or you can be more civil and crumble by hand.

When completely cooled, store whatever you have not already nibbled on in an airtight container where it will stay crisp for a week to 10 days.

SLÁINTE MUESLI

Muesli is oatmeal's daring, raw, naked cousin. With roots in the United Kingdom, it is one of the healthiest foods to hail from the British Isles! To that we say, "Sláinte!"—a toast to your good health in Gaelic, a language as old as oats!

Serves 2 or 3

1 cup old-fashioned oats

¼ cup raisins

3 dried apricots, finely diced

¼ cup dried cherries

2 tablespoons flaxseed meal

2 tablespoons chia seeds

½ cup Seed Bark Granola (page 35), optional; we love to add this crunch to the mix

Nondairy milk of choice (optional; my daughter prefers it dry)

Fresh fruit, for topping (optional)

In a medium bowl, toss together the oats, raisins, apricots, cherries, flaxseed meal, chia seeds, and Seed Bark Granola (if using). Portion the muesli into cereal bowls, pour on your favorite nondairy milk if you like, add berries or bananas on top, and dig in.

CURVE BALL OATMEAL

Throw that traditional oatmeal a curve ball with crispy, sweet, and filling additions.

Serves 1 or 2

1 cup cooked oatmeal (your choice—steel-cut or old-fashioned)

¼ cup Seed Bark Granola (page 35)

Handful raspberries or blueberries

½ banana, sliced

To the bowl of oatmeal, add the granola, berries, and banana. Dig in and watch your mood swing up and up.

SLÁINTE MUESLI

CURVE BALL OATMEAL

CRISP BAKED SURPRISE OATMEAL

This wonder of a breakfast was a surprise discovery! It was created in Amsterdam by someone who left their small pot of breakfast oatmeal on the stove for an hour, only to find an amazing, crispy-yet-moist, muffin-like treasure awaiting on their return! They passed the serendipitous recipe along to friends who passed it along to friends who passed it along to us. This is unlike any oatmeal breakfast we have ever had. We hope you discover what a treasure it is as well.

FOR FUN: Flip it out of the pan and knock on the external shell three times for good luck!

Serves 1 or 2

1 cup water

1 heaping cup old-fashioned oats

1 ¼ cups mixed fruit of choice (we recommend ½ banana, sliced; ½ ripe pear, diced; and ¼ peach or plum, diced)

Small handful berries (your choice)

1 tablespoon flaxseed meal, for garnish

In a small (about 1.25-quart) nonstick pot, mix together the water, oats, and fruit. It will look quite dry, and that is A-OK. Poke a handful of berries on top like candles.

Turn your gas stovetop on the lowest flame, or your electric stovetop on nearly the lowest flame—low/medium or, if it is numbered, 3 out of 10.

Cook uncovered for 1 hour. Yup, that is it. The oatmeal will be crispy on the sides and baked in the center.

Let the oatmeal cool for about 5 minutes before removing from the pan. Use a rubber spatula to free the sides, then help you slide the crisp creation out of the pan. If it is not yet crispy on the under-side, put it back over low heat (but a tiny bit higher heat than before) for 5 to 10 more minutes. All stovetops are different so you may have to play with the setting and exact timing to get the external shell crispy. Once it is out, admire this beauty, sprinkle with a little flaxseed meal, cut it in half to share with your breakfast partner, or eat it all yourself! Don't forget to knock on the crispy exterior three times for good luck!

LAP-IT-UP OATS

You will not regret the amount of food this recipe yields, the variety of flavors in your bowl, or how little time it takes before you're lapping it up with your favorite spoon.

Serves 1 or 2

1 cup water

½ cup old-fashioned oats

1 tablespoon chia seeds

½ banana, sliced

¼ cup blueberries

1 tablespoon almond butter

¼ cup Grape-Nuts cereal, or any nugget cereal (optional)

Bring the water to a boil in the microwave or on the stovetop. Meanwhile, place the oats and chia seeds in a breakfast bowl.

Pour the heated water over the oats and chia, cover with a plate, and let sit for about 5 minutes, until the oats and chia have fully absorbed the water.

Add the banana and blueberries, then stir in the almond butter. If you are in the mood for crunch, add the Grape-Nuts and hit the road!

It has been almost three months since we attended the Engine 2 Immersion in May of 2000. And honestly, if possible, we are even more committed to the program than we were when we left.

Howard is down 30 pounds since beginning the program and I am down 22 pounds. And yes, that is great, but the more important piece is what has happened on the inside— the things people don't see when they look at us. Howard had a heart attack in April 2000. That event led me to your dad's book and the Engine 2 Immersion program. Howard has severe heart disease (every male in his family has it). Cardiologists have told us there is nothing that can be done about it. Your diet is proof that something can be done about it! Howard's LDL the week before we arrived at Sedona was 151. After only two months of eating plant-strong, it was down to 36. His cardiologist ordered a scan of his carotid six weeks ago, saying every patient with heart disease has some plaque in his or her carotid and since Howard had had a heart event, he needed the scan to use as a baseline going forward. Howard saw the doctor after the scan and the doctor reported he had never seen anything like it. His carotid was completely clean!

Additionally, his blood pressure is consistently in the range of 106/68 (as is mine) and we both have so much energy and feel so great we are consistently exercising and planning activities with family and friends. Every meal at our house is plant-strong regardless of who is here!

I will be the first to tell you I am not a cook. In fact, I hated cooking! But the recipes in your books are so easy and delicious that I actually enjoy the cooking experience now.

Yes, we still have those skeptics in our lives who constantly ask us how we get our protein, so we simply respond (as Doug Lisle, author of *The Pleasure Trap*, suggested) that we have no idea. When those same skeptics tell us the diet is not balanced and we will eventually become ill, again we borrow Dr. Lisle's line and say it seems to be working for us so we are going to continue with it for now.

—KERRY AND HOWARD MERKUWITZ

SAVORY BREAKFAST OATS

Initially, this savory breakfast may seem "too new" or too different. Believe me when I tell you, we felt the same way. But then we tried it. Wow, does it grow on you! The nutritional yeast creates a wonderful creaminess. On a cold day, this warms you through and through. And you have the benefit of getting your greens at breakfast.

Once I accidentally used farro instead of oats (our grain cupboard is crowded!) and it was fantastic!

Serves 1 or 2

½ **cup steel-cut oats (or farro if you want to repeat my "experiment")**

1¾ **cups water**

2 **tablespoons nutritional yeast**

2 **cups chopped stemmed kale or greens of choice**

½ **cup sliced mushrooms (we love using shiitake, but any kind is delicious)**

3 **to 4 sundried tomatoes, thinly sliced**

¼ **teaspoon turmeric**

1 **teaspoon sriracha sauce or hot sauce of choice, or to taste**

1 **tablespoon chia seeds or flaxseed meal**

In a saucepan, combine the oats, water, nutritional yeast, kale, mushrooms, tomatoes (reserving some for garnish if you like), turmeric, and hot sauce. Bring just to a boil, watching carefully and stirring to prevent burning. Reduce the heat to maintain a simmer and cook, stirring occasionally, for 8 to 10 minutes; not all water will be absorbed when it is removed from the stove, but it thickens as it cools.

Sprinkle with sundried tomatoes, chia seeds, or flaxseed meal and feel the goodness.

50/50 HASH BROWNS

These hash browns are half white Yukon Gold potatoes and half orange sweet potatoes (unless you use Yellow Jersey sweet potatoes, which are white). *The key to the hash browns is to bake the potatoes the night before, so they can cool and set.* Then they are thoroughly cooked and easy to cut into cubes.

Serves 4

2 medium Yukon Gold potatoes

1 medium sweet potato

1 medium onion, diced

1 red bell pepper, diced

¼ teaspoon crushed black pepper, or to taste

3 shakes pepper flakes (optional)

Ketchup (no high-fructose corn syrup) and hot sauce, your choice (optional)

The night before you want to enjoy these delicious hash browns, preheat the oven to 400°F. Bake the Yukon Gold potatoes and the sweet potatoes for 40 minutes, or until cooked completely. Let cool in the fridge overnight.

In the morning, cube the potatoes—peeling the skin off is your choice. (We always leave the skin on!)

Heat a skillet over high heat. Add the onions and allow them to brown and soften while stirring, about 5 minutes. Add the cubed potatoes and diced bell pepper and cook until the potato cubes are browned and warmed through and through. Add the black pepper and pepper flakes, if using, and stir. Serve with ketchup and hot sauce, if you like.

KALE BLUEBERRY MUFFINS

These look like Dr. Seuss came over and baked with you—bright green muffins speckled with deep purple berries. If you are not turned away at the door, and curiosity gets the best of the critics, you will be the hit of the bake sale!

Makes 12 muffins

2 cups chopped stemmed kale

½ cup water

½ cup 100% pure maple syrup

2 tablespoons unsweetened applesauce

1 tablespoon apple cider vinegar

1 teaspoon vanilla extract

1½ cups oat flour, whole wheat flour, or gluten-free flour

1 teaspoon baking soda

1 teaspoon cinnamon

1 cup fresh blueberries

Preheat the oven to 350°F. Get out a 12-cup nonstick muffin pan. (We love our gold-colored muffin pan from Williams Sonoma, or use a silicone pan with a baking sheet beneath.)

Cook the kale in a pot with 1 to 2 inches of simmering water until the kale is dark green and soft.

Drain the kale (you should have about 1 cup) and add to a food processor along with the water, maple syrup, applesauce, vinegar, and vanilla. Blend until uniformly mixed—it will look like a green smoothie at this stage. Transfer the green goodness to a large mixing bowl.

Add the flour, baking soda, and cinnamon and stir. Add the blueberries and you are ready to scoop the batter into the muffin wells.

Bake the muffins for 18 minutes, until the tops are firm to the touch. These are best served warm, but will last for 5 days if stored in an airtight container.

APPLE-SAGE BREAKFAST PATTIES

Have a picky eater in your household? Or someone who prefers a savory breakfast over oatmeal? These breakfast patties will win them over without clogging their arteries. They go well over cooked spinach or greens—or make a bed of fresh greens instead. Top these flavor-filled patties with your preference of salsa, hot sauce, or a wee kiss of maple syrup.

Serves 3 to 5

8 to 12 ounces fresh spinach (depending on how much you like spinach)

1 (15-ounce) can cannellini beans, drained and rinsed

4 cloves garlic, minced

2 teaspoons low-sodium tamari

2 teaspoons dried sage

1 teaspoon dried rosemary

½ teaspoon fennel seeds

Pinch black pepper

Pinch white pepper

2 cups cooked red quinoa

¼ cup minced peeled apple

3 green onions, diced

TOPPINGS

Salsa, your favorite

Hot sauce, your favorite

1 tablespoon 100% pure maple syrup

Preheat the oven to 350°F. Line a baking sheet with parchment paper.

In a large pot over high heat, bring about 1 inch water to a boil. Add the spinach and steam for 3 minutes, or until cooked to your liking. Drain and set aside.

In a large skillet over medium heat, stir together the beans, garlic, tamari, sage, rosemary, fennel seeds, black pepper, and white pepper. Cook for 3 to 5 minutes, until fragrant and warm. Add water to the pan if the mixture gets too dry.

Add the cooked quinoa and apple and mix thoroughly. Stir vigorously—actually more like smash, smash, smash most of the beans until the mixture starts clumping. I often use my hands at this smashing stage. Add the green onions and stir again.

Using ¼ cup of the mixture for each, form 10 patties and place on the lined baking sheet.

Bake the patties for 15 minutes, until slightly browned on top. Serve the patties over a bed of the cooked spinach with salsa, hot sauce, or just a wee kiss of pure maple syrup.

FOLDED CHICKPEA OMELETS

This is a big taco-shaped omelet filled with spinach, mushrooms, onions, red peppers, and whatever other veggies you want to stuff inside. (See photo, page 26.)

Makes 2 (8- to 9-inch) omelets

1 medium onion, diced

½ cup diced mushrooms

2 cups packed fresh spinach

1 cup chickpea flour

⅓ cup nutritional yeast

½ teaspoon baking soda

½ teaspoon onion powder

½ teaspoon garlic powder

¼ teaspoon white pepper

¼ teaspoon black pepper

1 cup water

TOPPINGS

1 tomato, diced

Salsa, your favorite

Hot sauce, your favorite

In a skillet over high heat—so hot that a bead of water does not turn to steam, but rolls around on the surface—add the diced onions. Stir the onions as they brown, gradually turning the heat down to medium-high, for 3 to 5 minutes. Add the mushrooms and continue to cook and stir until the mushrooms are cooked through, 3 to 5 minutes longer. Add the spinach and continue to stir until the leaves wilt. Set the vegetables aside.

In a small bowl, combine the chickpea flour, nutritional yeast, baking soda, onion powder, garlic powder, white pepper, and black pepper. Add the water and stir until the batter is smooth.

In a skillet over medium heat, pour in half the batter to make an 8- to 9-inch pancake. Cook, sneaking little peeks at the bottom with the edge of the spatula, until the underside is browned, about 2 to 4 minutes as all burners vary. Flip the omelet like a pancake and cook for a minute or two, then check to see if the bottom side is cooked to your liking. We like the omelets to be soft like pancakes and slightly browned. Transfer the omelet to a plate with a large spatula. Place half of the cooked vegetables on one-half of the omelet, and fold the other half over like a taco!

Repeat to make a second omelet.

Serve with tomatoes and your favorite salsas and hot sauce.

GREEN HORNET TOAST

Start your day like a true superhero with this zippy, green breakfast. Go Green Hornet!

Serves 2

2 slices any variety of Ezekiel 4:9 bread, toasted (or 100% whole-grain bread of choice)
½ cup black beans
½ avocado, sliced or mashed
Salsa or hot sauce of choice

Toast the bread slices in a toaster. In a bowl, smash the black beans with the backside of a fork to make them stick together well and spread better. Spread the beans on the toast, top with the avocado, and add salsa or hot sauce to add some wake-up-some-zip to your morning!

I am a forty-three-year-old, soon to be forty-four-year-old, general surgeon who lives in Pawleys Island, S.C. I am the father of a three-year-old girl, Vivian, and a six-year-old son, Jon. My wife, Kelly, and I have led a fairly healthy-diet lifestyle for years, or what we thought was healthy. Being in the medical field and general surgery, I see the end results of our unhealthy society. My wife and I started a whole-plant-based diet approximately eight weeks ago. Both of us have felt the positive effects of healthier eating. I can say truly, I do not miss the burgers and fries. The food tastes better and I truly enjoy mealtime now. I have lost approximately 30 pounds, my cholesterol has improved, and my energy is off the charts. I have always known that I needed to eat healthier, but the information that I have received from you guys has helped me make that transition in a tasteful way.

Thank you for your information and guidance.

—MATTHEW J. METZ, MD

CHAPTER 4

SAUCES, SPREADS, SALSAS, DRESSINGS, DIPS, AND HUMMUS

ROMESCO SAUCE

This is a famous sauce from Spain where they do food right. Its flavor, texture, and subtle smoky flavor make it a favorite. We use Romesco sauce on pizza (page 203), over pasta, as part of our potato bar (page 236), in wraps, in grilled sandwiches (page 175), as a veggie dip...come to think of it, we use it everywhere!

Makes about 3 cups

2 ancient sweet red peppers (or red bell peppers)

2 medium tomatoes

2 cloves garlic, peeled

1 slice 100% whole-grain bread

½ cup slivered almonds

¼ cup hazelnuts

2 tablespoons balsamic vinegar

1 tablespoon smoked paprika

¼ teaspoon cayenne pepper

Black pepper, to taste

Preheat the oven to 450°F. Line a baking sheet with parchment paper.

Place the peppers, tomatoes, and garlic on the lined pan and roast, rotating occasionally, until the pepper skins blister and blacken, 20 to 30 minutes. Set aside.

Turn oven down to 350°F. Place the bread, almonds, and hazelnuts on a baking sheet and toast in the oven for 10 minutes, until browned and fragrant.

Once cooled, peel the tomatoes and peppers, and seed the peppers as well. Place the tomatoes, peppers, garlic, toasted bread, almonds, and hazelnuts in a food processor or high-speed blender along with the balsamic vinegar, paprika, cayenne, and black pepper. Blend until smooth like hummus, or to the texture you prefer.

Romesco can be made a day or so ahead of time—so make a huge batch, cover, and chill until ready to serve. You will never regret having extra to eat throughout the week.

OMG WALNUT SAUCE

This sauce will bring you to your knees. And don't be surprised if you come crawling back for more. It makes a great spread as well as a sauce.

Makes about 1½ cups

1 cup raw walnuts

2 cloves garlic, peeled

1 tablespoon low-sodium tamari

¼ to ½ cup water, for desired consistency

Combine the walnuts, garlic, and tamari in a food processor and blend, adding water until the desired texture is reached—more water for a thinner dressing, less for a thicker dip. (Adding the water is amazing to watch as the mixture miraculously turns from dark and chunky to white and creamy!) If you have any leftovers—we doubt you will—store in the fridge for up to five days.

Jalapeño Walnut Sauce and Spread: For a spicier variation, dial up the heat with as much jalapeño as you can handle: Seed and chop half a jalapeño pepper (or more), add to the blender, and blend it right in.

KALE BUTTER 3.0

The more we make this classic Engine 2 dip, the better it gets. Try a few dollops on top of your pizza for a change of pace. At our annual Plant-Stock event at the Esselstyn family farm in upstate New York, we had a special Friday dinner event for all the speakers and their families. We featured four new dips and all 50 people devoured this one first. Oh, kale yeah!

Makes about 4 cups

1 bunch kale, spines removed (equals about 4 cups kale leaves)
2 small or 1 large sweet potato
OMG Walnut Sauce (page 57)

Place the kale in a medium pot with a few inches of boiling water, cover, and cook for 4 to 5 minutes. Drain well; you should have about 2 cups.

Cook the sweet potato in whatever way works best for you until soft throughout: Bake in a 400°F oven for 45 minutes, or cook in the microwave for 8 minutes. Peel the sweet potato.

In a food processor or high-speed blender, combine the walnut sauce, cooked kale, and cooked sweet potato. Blend well—it becomes a beautiful, bright, full-bodied, green spread. Store any leftovers in a storage container in the fridge for up to 5 days.

BEET BUTTER

The color of beets is disarming: so beautiful, eye-catching, and bright. We like the high drama of a thick layer of purple Beet Butter on our Purple Haze Warrior Pockets (page 202) or in a Build-Your-Own Grilled Sandwich or Pita to Go (page 181).

Makes about 2½ cups

3 medium beets

2 large cloves garlic, peeled

½ cup walnuts

½ cup fresh parsley, coarsely chopped

1 tablespoon balsamic vinegar

1 tablespoon low-sodium tamari

1 teaspoon 100% pure maple syrup

½ teaspoon dried rosemary

¼ teaspoon turmeric

1 tablespoon to ½ cup water, your preference, for texture

Cook the beets in a large pot of boiling water for 30 minutes, or until soft inside. Let cool slightly, then rub off the skins under cold running water.

Combine the cooked beets, garlic, walnuts, parsley, vinegar, tamari, maple syrup, rosemary, and turmeric in a food processor and blend. Add water and blend until the desired texture is reached. Store any leftovers in a storage container in the fridge for up to 5 days.

SRIRACHA CARROT HUMMUS

The sriracha and carrot combo is fiery on the outside but very sweet at the core—just like us firefighters!

TIP: Cook ½ large sweet potato or one small sweet potato however you prefer: for about 8 minutes in the microwave, or about 45 minutes in a 400°F oven.

Makes about 3 cups

1 (15-ounce) can chickpeas, drained and rinsed

½ cup shredded carrots

½ ancient sweet red pepper (or red bell pepper), seeded

½ cup cooked sweet potato

3 tablespoons sriracha hot sauce

2 tablespoons 100% fruit apricot jam

2 cloves garlic, peeled

In a food processor or high-speed blender, combine the chickpeas, carrots, pepper, sweet potato, sriracha, jam, and garlic and blend. Use as a dip or spread it on thick!

SECRETARIAT SWEET CHILE SPREAD

This dip doesn't look like a champion. It is paler than its sandwich-spread cousins. But just like the racehorse Secretariat, it's a winner! The blend of beans and nuts, heat and sweet—with a hint of garlic and vinegar—has the spread outperforming any of its flashier competitors by a full body length. Spread on your sandwiches, pitas, and grilled wraps; add to your greens and salads; or use as a dip with vegetables or Pita Chips (page 131) and you are off to the races!

Makes about 1½ cups

½ cup canned cannellini beans, drained and rinsed

½ cup walnuts

4 teaspoons sriracha hot sauce, or your choice hot sauce

1 tablespoon rice vinegar

1 tablespoon 100% fruit apricot jam

1 clove garlic, peeled

In a food processor or high-speed blender, combine all the ingredients and blend until smooth. Taste and, if you prefer more heat, add another teaspoon of hot sauce. If you want it sweeter, add a teaspoon of apricot jam. If you want it smoother and not as thick, add a tablespoon of water. Make it to match your preference.

I'm a thirty-eight-year-old firefighter from Santa Cruz, California. The idea of doing a diet that was put together by a brother firefighter appealed to me. I'm 5 feet, 9 inches, and I now weigh in at 193 pounds. I sadly hit 230 pounds prior to implementing your diet plan. I have lost 37 pounds total and have spent a lot of money on new clothes. I haven't felt this good since I was in my early twenties. I have always been an athlete of sorts and very active, but I did not know how to eat very healthy. I felt because I ride my bike, surf, swim, and do boring workouts that didn't include core, squats, lunges, and dynamic workouts, that I was in good shape. Wrong! You really set the bar high for me and the results are too awesome to ignore. I just wanted to say thanks.

—LONO BARNES, FIREFIGHTER

THAI PEANUT BUTTER

This is an upgrade of a longtime childhood (and adult) favorite: peanut butter. Try on our Swee'Pea Grilled Sandwich (page 179) or Thai Flyin' Grilled Warrior Pockets (page 202), or on an open-faced sandwich with arugula, tomatoes, and fresh basil, or even over whole wheat pasta. You'll also enjoy it with vegetables and whole grains, not white bread and jelly—that's why we call this an upgrade!

Makes about 1½ cups

¼ cup natural peanut butter

1 cup canned cannellini beans, drained and rinsed

1 tablespoon minced fresh ginger

1 tablespoon low-sodium tamari

1 tablespoon 100% pure maple syrup

1 to 2 teaspoons hot sauce (we love sriracha, choose your preference for heat)

1 to 2 tablespoons water, your preference for texture

In a food processor or high-speed blender, combine all the ingredients and blend until smooth. Taste for your heat preference and add more hot sauce if needed.

KALE BUTTER 3.0
(page 58)

SRIRACHA CARROT HUMMUS
(page 62)

HOMEMADE HUMMUS
(page 67)

SECRETARIAT SWEET
CHILE SPREAD
(page 63)

THAI PEANUT BUTTER
(opposite)

BEET BUTTER
(page 61)

ROMESCO SAUCE
(page 54)

GINGER-WASABI
EDAMAME HUMMUS
(page 66)

THAI CURRY HUMMUS AND DIP
(page 69)

GINGER-WASABI EDAMAME HUMMUS

As an old friend of mine, Steve Tarpinian, used to say, "the beauty is in the balance." This hummus is a beautiful balance of heat, sweet, zing, and hum. Make the spread to suit your taste—more heat, more sweet, or more toasted seeds—your call!

Makes about 1¾ cups

1½ cups shelled edamame

¼ cup pickled ginger

2 cloves garlic, peeled

¼ cup water (we often use the vinegar from the pickled ginger jar instead of water for more zing!)

3 tablespoons fresh lemon juice

1½ to 3 teaspoons wasabi powder, depending on how hot you want it

¼ cup sesame seeds

In a food processor or high-speed blender, combine the edamame, ginger, garlic, water, lemon juice, and wasabi powder. Blend until well incorporated.

In a skillet over medium heat, toast the sesame seeds for 5 to 8 minutes, until lightly browned and fragrant.

Add the sesame seeds to the food processor while still sizzling hot—this infuses a toasted sesame flavor into the hummus. Blend again until the sesame seeds are spread throughout the hummus.

Give the hummus a taste. If you prefer more heat, add more wasabi powder. If you want more of the toasted seed flavor, add more toasted sesame seeds. Or if you seek more of the sweet zingy taste of the ginger, add more pickled ginger—it's your call. Serve immediately or chill until ready to serve.

HOMEMADE HUMMUS

We eat so much hummus, it's a constantly evolving recipe with many variations. This is a slight upgrade from the original hummus recipe in our first book, *The Engine 2 Diet*.

Makes about 1¼ cups

1 (15-ounce) can chickpeas, drained and rinsed

2 cloves garlic, peeled

2 tablespoons lemon juice

2 teaspoons mustard, your favorite

1 teaspoon low-sodium tamari

¼ teaspoon ground cumin

¼ teaspoon turmeric

2 teaspoons water, or more for desired consistency

In a food processor or high-speed blender, combine the chickpeas, garlic, lemon juice, mustard, tamari, cumin, and turmeric and blend until smooth. Add water and blend to reach desired texture.

Hey Man! Got to thank you. Few months back I heard you speak and you were saying the first sign of heart disease was ED. Well I didn't want to admit it, but let's just say things in that department were not rock solid like they used to be. I could get it up, but it just wasn't really that UP, not like I'd like it to be, anyway. I thought it was just getting older, because I thought I was eating healthy—eating crap like coconut oil, meat, more meat—and I had lost weight, so I ignored it. I couldn't shake the feeling that there was something to what you said, even though my paleo friends said you were off your rocker. Went to the doctor and found out I was in BAD shape. Had no clue! I'm only 32! What the hell? Heart disease? So my doctor tells me how it just runs in my family, which I called bullshit on. I go on your eating plan, cut out all of the flesh and cow milk. So it's now 2 months. My doctor said that my cholesterol dropped 70 points: yeah, great, whatever. But you know what stopped dropping? That's right buddy. Everything in that department is flying high and proud. I feel like I have superhuman strength. I could balance on it. I had been on paleo for a while, got a little thinner, but turns out that going paleo makes your penis, sad-eo. Bring on the healthy carbs, the potatoes, the bean burgers, the fruit! Guys need to know they definitely won't get more manly with meat. Thanks man, I owe you one!

—MICHAEL

GARLIC LOVER'S HUMMUS

For thousands of years, garlic has been hailed for its amazing properties. The Olympic athletes in ancient Greece may have used it as the first "performance enhancing" agent in sports. Today garlic is known for its ability to fight off colds, infection, creepy dates, and vampires. Spread it on your favorite sandwich tonight, and save going on that date for tomorrow.

Makes about 1¼ cups

1 large or 2 small bulbs garlic

1 cup (8 ounces) Homemade Hummus (page 67) or store-bought hummus with no added oil or tahini

Preheat the oven to 350°F.

With a knife or sharp scissors, cut off the top (the pointed part) of the bulbs of garlic and place the bulbs cut-side up in a small baking pan that can be covered (we use a clay garlic baker). Cover and bake for about 1 hour, until the bulbs of garlic are caramelized and soft to the touch. Remove from the oven and let cool.

Squeeze the garlic pulp out of the cloves (I love this part!) and collect in a bowl. Add 6 to 8 cloves baked garlic to the hummus and stir until well combined. If you want a smoother texture, blend the garlic and hummus in a food processor or high-speed blender until the desired texture is reached.

THAI CURRY HUMMUS AND DIP

CAUTION: Use of this hummus will change that same old sandwich into a magic carpet ride.

Makes about 1¼ cups

1 cup (8 ounces) Homemade Hummus (page 67) or store-bought hummus with no added oil or tahini

1 tablespoon green curry paste (we prefer Thai Kitchen brand)

1 teaspoon 100% pure maple syrup

¼ teaspoon coconut extract

Combine the hummus, curry paste, maple syrup, and coconut extract in a high-speed blender or food processor and mix until well combined.

HATCH GREEN CHILE HUMMUS

Chiles from Hatch, New Mexico, are seasonal and hard to find. However, they are so worth it. As they say, once you go Hatch you never go back. Their flavor and unique heat are addictive.

Makes 1½ cups

¼ cup to ½ cup roasted Hatch green chiles (to your taste)

1 cup (8 ounces) Homemade Hummus (page 67)

In a food processor or high-speed blender, combine the roasted chiles and hummus and blend until you reach your desired texture. We like to see a few chiles in the mix, others like it smooth. Do your thing and enjoy it on your sandwiches or as a dip or spread.

CORN CHIPS OR RICE CHIPS
(page 132)

SOCO GUACAMOLE

Rip was introduced to this guacamole at a party in a 1924 bungalow that was purchased from the Sears Roebuck catalogue in the eclectic South Congress (SoCo) district of ATX (Austin, Texas). Rip's eaten a lot of guacamole in his days and this was off the charts. Try with our Corn Chips (page 132).

Makes about 3 cups

2 ripe avocados

½ cup cilantro, chopped

½ cup finely diced onion

½ to 1 jalapeño pepper (depending on how much heat you seek), seeded and diced

1 tomato, seeded and chopped

1 tablespoon fresh lime juice

1 clove garlic, finely minced

½ cup sugar snap peas, diced (optional)

In a bowl, combine all the ingredients. Use a fork to mix, smash, and stir until it is the consistency of your choice—some like it chunkier, some like it smoother.

LOVELY SAUCE

So rich, so green, so lovely. Wendy, the creative force behind this sauce, has *LOVELY* tattooed across her broad shoulders. Just watch, after you top any dish or bowl with the sauce, you'll notice the dance of the deep, authentic flavors while your toes tap, your hips subtly sway, and your taste buds say "lovely." Serve like you would your favorite salsa: as a dip, as a topping, added to recipes, to burritos (page 238), even layered on top of Deck Gun Nachos (page 122) for sure!

Makes about 3 cups

4 bunches cilantro, large stems removed (4 to 5 cups)

1 medium sweet onion, chopped

1 avocado, pitted and peeled

½ jalapeño pepper, seeded

4 cloves garlic, minced

Juice of 1 lemon (about 2 tablespoons)

Juice of 1 lime (about 2 tablespoons)

2 teaspoons 100% pure maple syrup

½ teaspoon ground cumin

Combine all the ingredients in a food processor and blend until smooth.

ASIAN FUSION SAUCE

We are huge fans of Asian flavor profiles in sauces and dressings. And apparently so is our neighbor. After tasting this dressing at our house late one afternoon, he went home, prepared his own dinner of rice and veggies, and then came back to our house to retrieve the dressing for dinner back at his place!

Inspiration for this dressing comes from Rouxbe, an online plant-based cooking school. We added a texture boost with the toasted sesame seeds. Use this as you would any teriyaki sauce, or serve over rice and veggies, on salads, over soba noodles, or even baked on tofu.

Makes generous 1 cup

2 tablespoons low-sodium tamari

2 tablespoons mirin (Japanese sweet rice wine)

1 tablespoon vegan Worcestershire sauce

1 tablespoon red curry paste

1 tablespoon 100% pure maple syrup

1 tablespoon water

2 tablespoons sesame seeds, toasted in a dry skillet until lightly browned and fragrant

In a small food processor or high-speed blender, combine all the ingredients and blend until well blended and smooth.

LO MEIN NOODLE SAUCE

Our kids clamor for lo mein noodles whenever ordering Chinese food, which motivated me to make a healthier version. We officially love this sauce! I cannot say that it is officially Lo Mein Noodle Sauce, but I can say that it is officially great.

Makes 1½ cups

⅓ cup sesame seeds, toasted in a dry skillet until lightly browned and fragrant

⅓ to ½ cup walnuts

⅓ cup low-sodium tamari

⅓ cup pure 100% pure maple syrup

1 tablespoon minced fresh ginger

2 tablespoons water

½ teaspoon sriracha, or more to taste (optional)

In a food processor or high-speed blender, combine all the ingredients and blend until smooth and uniform in texture.

ASIAN FUSION SAUCE
(page 73)

LO MEIN NOODLE SAUCE
(opposite)

LICK-THE-BOWL PEANUT
SAUCE (page 76)

LICK-THE-BOWL PEANUT SAUCE

Our brother Ted said he licked the bowl after making this sauce from Isa Chandra Moskowitz's amazing book, *Isa Does It.* We are huge fans of Isa, and of Ted, and of peanut sauce—so we had to try making this one plant-strong. If you think you may prefer this without the curry (Ted loves the curry), we're sure Ted won't mind. Spoon over rice, whole wheat pasta, potatoes, sweet potatoes, or greens!

Makes about 2 cups

1½ tablespoons minced fresh ginger

3 cloves garlic, minced

1 cup water

⅔ cup natural peanut butter

2 tablespoons rice vinegar

2 tablespoons low-sodium tamari

2 tablespoons 100% pure maple syrup

2 teaspoons curry powder (optional)

1 teaspoon hot sauce (we use sriracha)

In a small saucepan over medium heat, combine the ginger and garlic and cook and stir for about 2 minutes, until the ingredients get fragrant and stick to the bottom of the pan. Add the water and continue to cook, lifting anything sticking to the bottom of the pan, for another minute.

Add the peanut butter, vinegar, tamari, maple syrup, curry (if using), and hot sauce and continue stirring until everything gets warm, smooth, and saucy. Serve immediately or refrigerate until ready to use.

CLEAN AND CLASSIC RED MARINARA

We never thought before to make our own pasta sauce. But as our guideline of no added oil made it more difficult to find a compliant sauce, we started making our own. It is so quick and easy. This is our newest incarnation of marinara. It makes a ton, feeds a crowd, fills a lasagna, and tastes fresher than any jarred sauce out there.

TIP: Add anything you like to the sauce: caramelized onions, cooked mushrooms, bell peppers, zucchini, or other veggies you love.

Makes 7 cups

1 (6-ounce) can tomato paste

1 (28-ounce) can crushed tomatoes, no salt added

1 (28-ounce) can petite diced tomatoes, no salt added

2 tablespoons 100% pure maple syrup

2 tablespoons 100% fruit apricot jam

1 tablespoon dried basil

1 tablespoon dried oregano

2 teaspoons dried thyme

1 teaspoon onion powder

1 teaspoon garlic powder

¼ teaspoon crushed red pepper flakes

¼ teaspoon cayenne pepper

In a shallow saucepan over medium-high heat, cook the tomato paste, without stirring, to the point where it almost burns, about 3 minutes, then stir. Add the crushed tomatoes, diced tomatoes, maple syrup, jam, basil, oregano, thyme, onion powder, garlic powder, red pepper flakes, and cayenne pepper and continue to stir and simmer for 3 to 4 minutes. Decrease the heat to low and simmer for 5 to 10 minutes longer, until the ingredients are warm throughout. Serve warm over pasta and/or vegetables.

TRUE GRIT GRAVY

The Grit vegetarian restaurant in Athens, Georgia, is on our bucket list because of their amazing cookbook, *The Grit Cookbook* (by Jessica Greene and Ted Hafer). It is a bible in many vegetarian kitchens. We have changed their gravy recipe a bit here to be true to our gritty plant-strong guidelines. The gravy smells like Thanksgiving or a savory meal at a tavern and is fantastic with anything, but we suggest Beer Biscuits (page 119) for dunking.

Makes about 3 cups

1 large sweet onion, diced

8 ounces mushrooms, sliced

3 tablespoons whole wheat flour or oat flour

1 tablespoon nutritional yeast

½ teaspoon ground sage

¼ teaspoon white pepper

Pinch dry mustard

1 tablespoon white miso

About 2 cups water, your preference for texture (note: the gravy thickens as it cools)

2 tablespoons low-sodium tamari

In a skillet over medium-high heat, cook the onion, stirring continuously, until translucent, 3 to 5 minutes. Add the mushrooms and continue cooking until they are cooked thoroughly. Remove the pan from the heat completely and add the flour, nutritional yeast, sage, white pepper, and dry mustard. Stir all the ingredients so they are well coated.

Dissolve the miso in the water. Return the pan to medium-low heat and add the miso water and tamari. Cook and stir continuously over heat until the gravy thickens, about 5 minutes. Please keep in mind that it thickens a bit as it cools—so be sure to add enough water as I have found this gravy spreadable the next day! If you want to make it smoother, send it through the food processor or high-speed blender before serving.

SMOKY BAKE-ON MARINADE

You have to pronounce *Bake-On* as "bacon"! The familiar Bake-On smoky flavor adds a flare of flavor to ingredients in your sandwich, burrito, salad, or pizza. This Smoky Bake-On Marinade flavors the tempeh or tofu perfectly in our favorite sandwich, BLT&A (page 168).

Makes ½ cup

¼ cup low-sodium tamari

¼ cup water

1 tablespoon hot sauce, your favorite (we prefer Cholula)

1 teaspoon liquid smoke

In a bowl, mix together the tamari, water, hot sauce, and liquid smoke. Store in an airtight container or use as a marinade right away.

To use the Bake-On Marinade: Cut ¼-inch-thick slices of zucchini, eggplant, tempeh, or tofu. Add the marinade and soak for at least 15 minutes. Place the slices on a parchment-lined baking sheet and bake in a 350°F oven for 30 to 45 minutes—the longer the slices cook the chewier they get. Place these tasty slices on sandwiches, in your burritos, chopped up in salads, or add to Folded Chickpea Omelets (page 50).

> You changed my life and I'm certain you saved my life. I was headed down a dangerous path with my eating habits that most likely would have led to heart disease and health problems. I was 200 pounds, unhealthy, and a drive-thru junkie. I committed to being plant-strong for 28 days in January of 2012 and have been plant-strong ever since! I went from a sedentary lifestyle to completing three half-marathons, joining a gym, running, and doing yoga. What a difference! My husband is also plant-strong, we're raising our two kids plant-strong, and my in-laws have jumped on board too. This is a way of life for us now. I lost 50 pounds, my husband lost 30 pounds, and he is now completely diabetes free and off all medication. His endocrinologist was stupefied and couldn't believe he had reversed his diabetes. You are capable of change if you choose it. We chose to change our lives and be plant-strong!
>
> —ALLISON LYON, MOM

EAST SIDE SALSA

Here's a little trick that will help you find a house address: In most cities, if the end of the address is an odd number it will be on the south or east side of the street. If it ends in an even number it will be on the north or west side. When driving the fire engine this trick always made it easier to find the house. Our neighbors who live on the east side of the street brought this salsa to a pool party and we dug everything about it: All the elements are chunky, nothing is smooshed up—everything is cubed and chopped and each ingredient is visible.

Makes 2 to 3 cups

1 avocado, cubed

½ red onion, finely chopped

½ bunch fresh cilantro, coarsely chopped (½ to ¾ cup)

1 cup canned pinto beans, drained and rinsed

1 medium tomato, chopped

1 tablespoon white vinegar

1 tablespoon fresh lime juice

Salt, to taste (optional)

In a bowl, combine all the ingredients and gently toss together so nothing gets smooshed too much. Serve with anything and everything!

ROASTED CORN SALSA

This blend of old favorites draws out strong flavors. Lime and peppers elevate the sweetness of the corn with its rustic roasted undertone, and the onions and black pepper throw down a slam dunk. This salsa will be a huge hit. If we do not have any roasted corn, we use frozen sweet corn, which works just as well.

Makes 2 cups

1 cup corn, roasted, frozen, or off the cob

¼ cup cilantro, loosely chopped

⅓ cup finely diced red bell pepper

¼ cup finely diced sweet onion

½ jalapeño pepper, minced; or 1 poblano pepper, seeded and diced

Grated zest of 1 lime

2 tablespoons fresh lime juice

Black pepper, to taste

In a bowl, combine all the ingredients. Stir and taste to see if you want to tweak it with more lime, cilantro, or black pepper, and serve.

MIGHTY MANGO SALSA
(page 86)

PICO DE GALLO
(page 87)

ROASTED CORN SALSA
(opposite)

MIGHTY MANGO SALSA

Mango is the number one consumed fruit in the world! The color, the flavor, the medley of tastes have us serving this salsa more than any other. Hands down.

Makes about 2 cups

2 small or 1 large ripe mango, diced

¼ red onion, minced

½ cup fresh parsley or cilantro

Grated zest of 1 lime

Juice of 1½ limes (about 3 tablespoons)

In a bowl, combine all the ingredients and mix. Serve over anything that needs a lift!

BRANDO MANGO SALSA

If you've ever seen the movie *Apocalypse Now,* you'll recall that Marlon Brando was sucking on ripe mangoes while hiding in the shadows. We bet he would love this salsa.

Makes 2½ cups

1 fresh mango, cubed, or 1½ cups frozen mango cubes

⅓ cup diced red bell pepper

½ cup small-diced pineapple

¼ cup small-diced red onion

2 to 3 tablespoons fresh lime juice

1 teaspoon seeded and minced jalapeño pepper

Chopped fresh cilantro, to taste (optional)

In a bowl, combine the mango, bell pepper, pineapple, red onion, lime juice, jalapeño, and cilantro if using. Serve immediately or keep in the refrigerator until ready to serve.

PICO DE GALLO

This is a simple traditional Mexican salsa fresca made from tomatoes, onion, and jalapeños. *Pico,* as the dish is affectionately called, pairs perfectly with Mexican dishes such as our Exploding Burrito Bar (page 238) and Award-Winning Black Beans (page 229), adding a nice amount of flavor and freshness!

Makes 2 cups

2 medium-size tomatoes, diced

¼ cup diced white onion

½ fresh jalapeño pepper, seeded and diced

1 tablespoon minced garlic

2 lemons, juiced (3 to 4 tablespoons)

¼ cup cilantro, finely chopped

In a bowl, combine all the ingredients and stir. Serve freshly made or chilled.

BRANDO MANGO SALSA
(page 86)

CRANBERRY SALSA
(opposite)

EL NORTE SALSA
(page 90)

CRANBERRY SALSA

In some people's minds, cranberries are only for Thanksgiving. Not us. We serve these vitamin C–bearing bombs year-round in the form of this crazy-good salsa. Serve as part of our Exploding Burrito Bar (page 238) or Full House Potato Bar (page 236), or with our Award-Winning Black Beans (page 229).

TIP: Blending longer turns the salsa into more of a relish, which can also be delish!

Makes 2½ to 3 cups

1 (12-ounce) package fresh or frozen cranberries

3 to 4 green onions, thinly sliced

2 cups fresh cilantro (measured whole, without stems, not chopped)

½ large jalapeño pepper, seeded and chopped

3 tablespoons fresh lime juice

½ to ¾ cup 100% pure maple syrup, to taste

Combine all the ingredients in a food processor and blend only until coarsely chopped. Chill and serve.

EL NORTE SALSA

Salsa is not always a hot Southwestern favorite—we Northerners can do it right as well.

Makes about 3 cups

1 green apple, diced

6 ounces fresh or frozen cranberries

1 mango, peeled and diced

¼ red onion, minced

½ cup fresh parsley

Grated zest of 1 lime

Juice of 1 lime (about 2 tablespoons)

2 to 3 tablespoons 100% pure maple syrup (optional)

½ jalapeño pepper, seeded and diced (optional)

Place all the ingredients in a food processor and blend until the salsa reaches a chunky, relish-like texture.

About two years ago I was as big as I had ever been, around 325 pounds. I was in my forties and my genetics and lifestyle did not bode well.

After learning about how my future health was in my control, I knew I had to go "all in" and become truly plant-strong! Everything changed. Weight began to fall off easily and my energy, skin, sleep, thinking, and mood all got remarkably better. Now I rarely get sick; my allergies don't seem to exist anymore. I could go on and on. My doctor couldn't believe my results in a year. I weighed 219 pounds, my cholesterol had gone from 230ish down to under 120, and my blood pressure, which was "borderline" high, was 110/55 with a resting HR of around 50. My doc asked what I had done. I said I have become plant-based and spoke of you and your father. He said that's great but I should really have a little lean meat or fish. I responded, "What in my test results indicates that?" He looked at them again and said, "Just keep doing what you're doing, I'm going to be bragging to the other docs and patients about you and what can be achieved!" I have gone from near stent to getting ready to run the Cherry Blossom Ten Mile Run and from someone who was dying to someone who really lives life now!

—JASON SIGLER

LIGHTNING DRESSING

Here it is, lightning in a bottle! Get struck and be forever changed. There is depth, heat, and power in this beautifully balanced dressing. Serve over salad, greens, or grains—or check out the Green Lightning Bowl (page 199).

Makes about 1 cup

5 tablespoons low-sodium tamari

5 tablespoons 100% pure maple syrup

2 tablespoons rice vinegar

1 clove garlic, minced

2 teaspoons finely minced fresh ginger

½ jalapeño pepper, seeded and diced

Grated zest of 1 lime

Juice of 1 lime (about 2 tablespoons)

3 shakes red pepper flakes

In a small lidded container, combine all the ingredients. Place the lid on tightly and shake, shake, shake: That lightning needs to get all fired up.

SANDY'S CAESAR DRESSING

This traditional Caesar knockoff comes to us from an Engine 2 plant-strong advocate, Sandy Spallino, who credits Miyoko Schinner for the inspiration. We thank everyone involved for creating this Caesar dressing without eggs, anchovies, and oil! Try this on our "Kale, Caesar!" Salad (page 136) or toss with romaine lettuce and add Homemade Croutons (page 152) to serve.

Makes about 1 cup

3 tablespoons nutritional yeast

3 tablespoons Dijon mustard

2 tablespoons almond meal (also called almond flour)

3 cloves garlic, finely minced or pressed through a garlic press

¼ cup water

3 tablespoons fresh lemon juice

2 tablespoons low-sodium tamari

½ teaspoon vegan Worcestershire sauce

⅓ teaspoon freshly ground black pepper

In a medium bowl, combine the nutritional yeast, mustard, almond meal, and garlic to make a paste. Whisk in the water, lemon juice, tamari, Worcestershire sauce, and black pepper.

TERIYAKI SAUCE AND DRESSING

Sauce or dressing—it's your choice! (Note: The dressing is made by running the sauce through the food processor.) The dressing actually came into existence when Engine 2 chef Brenda Reed blended leftover teriyaki sauce in the food processor to make a fuller-bodied dressing. It has ever more become a staple dressing at all the Engine 2 Immersion events. We always double or triple this sauce to use on Killer Kabobs (page 230), Terrific Teriyaki Tofu Bowl (page 186), or to just have on hand.

Makes about ¾ cup

5 tablespoons low-sodium tamari

3 tablespoons 100% pure maple syrup

1 tablespoon tomato paste or ketchup (no high-fructose corn syrup)

2 teaspoons minced fresh ginger

2 tablespoons sesame seeds, toasted in a dry skillet until lightly browned and until fragrant

In a small bowl, combine the tamari, maple syrup, tomato paste, ginger, and sesame seeds. Use the sauce to marinate tofu.

To make a dressing: Blend the sauce in a food processor or high-speed blender for about 3 minutes, until uniformly smooth and fragrant. Use the dressing on salad, in a stir-fry, or tossed in soba noodle salads.

DRAGON DRESSING

Jane's son Zeb had a favorite children's book, *Herb the Vegetarian Dragon,* by Jules Bass and Debbie Harter. It is a light-hearted twist on traditional fairy tales with an empathetic, garden-tending, young dragon, Herb, who refuses to eat knights and destroy villages like his fellow dragons. You will love the story as well as our Herb-approved dressing, which is great on any salad, greens, grains, or as a dip!

Makes about 1 cup

½ cup natural peanut butter (use fresh ground if you can find it)

3 tablespoons rice vinegar

2 tablespoons low-sodium tamari

1 to 2 tablespoons 100% pure maple syrup

1 tablespoon hot sauce, your favorite (we love sriracha)

2 cloves garlic, peeled

1½ teaspoons minced fresh ginger

⅓ cup water, or more, depending on the texture you prefer

In a small food processor or high-speed blender, combine the peanut butter, vinegar, tamari, maple syrup, hot sauce, garlic, ginger, and water. Add more water for a thinner and smoother texture and less for a thicker texture. Blend until all the ingredients are smooth and dressing-like.

HEALTHY OR MANLY?

Rip overheard a strong, stocky man walk up to the pizza counter at the University Whole Foods store in Providence and order a slice of pizza. The woman behind the counter asked which kind: cheese, cheese and pepperoni, or one of three different types of vegan options? He looked at her aghast and said, "Oh no, I'm not going there, those are way too healthy! Give me the cheese and pepperoni." Rip had to do a plant-strong intervention. As he tells the story:

I approached and asked why the vegan options were too healthy for him. He said he was more interested in eating manly than eating healthy. I looked him up and down and replied how interesting it was that he was more compelled to make his choice based upon what was perceived as being a masculine food rather than a healthy food. In my opinion, the strongest, healthiest, and manliest foods on the planet are the plant-based foods with all of their miraculous qualities to protect us from disease: healthy protein, unprocessed carbohydrates that are our bodies primary fuel source, essential fatty acids, fiber, antioxidants (64 times more in plants than animals), and phytonutrients (which only exist in plants). I told him the manly way to eat was to eat these foods and become lean and mean and bulletproof to Western disease and to be healthy for himself, his family, and to set an example for his friends. Hey, the truth is real men don't care what others think as long as it's the right move. So man up and get that cheese-less pizza with arugula, bell peppers, pomegranate seeds, balsamic glaze, garlic, caramelized onions, grilled tofu, sweet potatoes, and black-eyed peas. You deserve it. And it's the manliest pizza of the lot! Let's just say he ended up making the right call!

ETERNAL DRESSING

Our mother brought this dressing over one beautiful, cool, and crisp Cleveland evening and we could not stop complimenting her on how amazing it was. Again and again and again we lathered on the compliments until finally she succumbed and shared the recipe for this eternal beauty. BTW, you ginger lovers will adore this!

Makes about ½ cup

2 tablespoons Homemade Hummus (page 67) or store-bought hummus with no added oil or tahini

2 tablespoons lemon vinegar (try to find a high quality lemon/citrus vinegar)

Juice of ½ lime (about 1 tablespoon)

1 teaspoon minced fresh ginger

½ teaspoon mustard, your favorite

¼ teaspoon turmeric

2 to 3 tablespoons water, or more, to desired texture

In a small bowl, combine all the ingredients and whisk with a fork until well combined. Serve!

COLLEGE DRESSING

Ever heard the expression, "Give it the old college try"? It means to give it your best shot. Jane's husband, Brian, did his best with this dressing and we think it deserves an A+.

Makes 1 cup

⅓ cup orange balsamic vinegar (or any light-colored, citrus-infused vinegar)

¼ cup mustard, your choice

2 tablespoons 100% pure maple syrup

2 teaspoons finely minced garlic

Combine all the ingredients in a medium bowl and use an immersion blender to mix until frothy and fragrant.

MANGO LEMON DRESSING

This recipe delivers a zing to your taste buds while adding body to your salad.

Makes about 1¼ cups

1 mango, peeled and diced

2 tablespoons fresh lemon juice

2 tablespoons rice vinegar

2 teaspoons chia seeds

Pinch of freshly ground black pepper, to taste

A squirt or two of hot sauce (we prefer sriracha)

In a small food processor or high-speed blender, combine the mango, lemon juice, vinegar, and chia seeds and blend until well combined. Season with black pepper and hot sauce, stir a bit more, and serve.

ANN AND ESSY'S FAVORITE

This dressing is what our parents, Ann and Essy, enjoy on their salad six out of seven nights a week. Really. It is a no-brainer for them. Do what they did: Find a dressing that works for you and dial it in as often as you'd like!

Makes ½ cup

2 tablespoons Homemade Hummus (page 67) or store-bought hummus with no added oil or tahini

A hint of grated orange zest

2 tablespoons fresh orange juice, or ½ orange including sections and juice

2 tablespoons balsamic vinegar

2 teaspoons mustard, your favorite

1 teaspoon minced fresh ginger

In a small bowl, combine all the ingredients with a fork. Toss onto your salad and serve.

TERIYAKI DRESSING
(page 93)

GINGER, WALNUT,
AND MISO DRESSING
(page 100)

SWEET FIRE DRESSING
(page 101)

ETERNAL DRESSING
(page 96)

DRAGON DRESSING
(page 94)

ANN AND ESSY'S
FAVORITE (page 97)

COLLEGE DRESSING
(page 96)

RIP'S FAVORITE RANCH
(opposite)

SANDY'S CAESAR
DRESSING (page 92)

AMAZON DRESSING
(page 101)

LIGHTNING DRESSING
(page 91)

RIP'S FAVORITE RANCH

I never ate salads as a kid. Never. I remember the first salad I ever had was at a restaurant when I was a freshman in high school. I ordered the same thing as my swim coach, Jim Starrett. Included with the main dish was a plain salad with ranch dressing. I remember loving the dressing and thinking I could eat any salad as long as it had a dressing this good on top. Well, this dressing is just as good and a ton better for you! Thanks to Erin Vesey for the recipe.

Makes 1¼ cups

¼ cup raw cashews

1 cup almond milk

1 to 2 tablespoons fresh lemon juice

1 small shallot, minced (or ¼ cup minced onion)

1 heaping tablespoon minced fresh parsley

1 heaping tablespoon finely chopped fresh chives

1 teaspoon garlic powder

1 teaspoon onion powder

1 teaspoon dried dill

⅛ teaspoon salt, to taste (optional)

Fresh black pepper, to taste

Ideally the night before, or for at least 30 minutes before preparing the recipe, soak the cashews in the almond milk.

Place the cashews and almond milk, the lemon juice, shallots, parsley, chives, garlic powder, onion powder, dill, salt, and pepper in a high-speed blender and blend until smooth. Serve immediately or store in the fridge.

GINGER, WALNUT, AND MISO DRESSING

As the saying goes, "The whole is greater than the sum of its parts." This intriguing dressing was created in that classic hit-or-miss fashion of combining two favorites and coming up with an even better favorite. Enjoy your salads, grains, and greens anointed with this winner of a dressing!

Makes about 1 cup

⅓ cup walnuts

1 clove garlic, minced

⅓ cup rice vinegar

2 tablespoons miso (we prefer white miso)

2 tablespoons 100% pure maple syrup

1 tablespoon finely minced fresh ginger

2 teaspoons low-sodium tamari, or to taste

2 to 4 tablespoons water

Blend all the ingredients in a food processor, adding the amount of water you prefer to reach desired texture, and serve.

SWEET FIRE DRESSING

The balance of flavor and heat in this winner of a dressing will leave your taste buds stunned and amazed. At our weeklong Sedona Engine 2 Immersions, the participants line up to sauce their greens with this special blend. It only takes one bite to be hooked on the sweet, hot awesomeness!

Makes 1 cup

½ cup plain oat milk

¼ cup Dijon mustard or spicy brown mustard, your choice

¼ cup 100% pure maple syrup

½ teaspoon cayenne pepper, or less if you don't like much heat

⅛ teaspoon smoked paprika

Combine all the ingredients in a bowl, stir well, and serve.

AMAZON DRESSING

This gem from the jungle adds swing to any salad. It's big on flavor and the mango gives it a tropical twist.

Makes about 1 cup

3 tablespoons fresh lime juice

1 mango, peeled and pitted

2 green onions, chopped

2 tablespoons chopped fresh cilantro or basil

1 tablespoon minced fresh jalapeño pepper

½ teaspoon ground cumin

In a food processor or blender, combine all the ingredients and blend until smooth.

BLOCK PARTY SPINACH AND ARTICHOKE DIP

Our version of the famous spinach dip did not have artichokes in it until a friend announced, "Heck, I throw a jar of artichokes in with the spinach. And I love to use frozen spinach—so easy. I serve it at home with home-toasted whole wheat pita chips. At our block party it is a huge hit with mini whole wheat pitas." So: Serve with Pita Chips (page 131), or veggies.

Makes 3 to 4 cups

2 ripe avocados, pitted and peeled

¼ cup diced onion

2 large cloves garlic, peeled

½ jalapeño pepper, seeded

3 tablespoons nutritional yeast

2 tablespoons fresh lemon juice

1 tablespoon white miso paste

1 tablespoon low-sodium tamari

1 teaspoon onion powder

½ teaspoon hot sauce, your choice

1 (10-ounce) package frozen chopped spinach

1 (14-ounce) jar artichokes, drained, rinsed, and squeezed of extra water

In a food processor or high-speed blender, combine the avocado, onion, garlic, jalapeño, nutritional yeast, lemon juice, miso, tamari, onion powder, and hot sauce and blend until smooth. Add the spinach and artichokes and blend to incorporate them into the mixture. When the texture is to your preference, place in a storage container and chill until ready to serve.

QUICK BLUEBERRY TOPPING

Fresh or frozen berries work for this sweet topping. We use a lemon press to get the juice out of the clementines. Don't have any clementines or oranges? Substitute unsweetened orange juice. Serve and enjoy on Sunday Morning Blueberry Pancakes (page 28), Sedona Sweet Potato Waffles (page 31), Big Hit Waffles (page 32), or in your oatmeal.

Makes about 1 cup

1½ cups blueberries, fresh or frozen (in our house we use the ones that are too soft for the picky kids)

Juice of 2 clementines or small oranges (again, in our house we use the ones that are too soft for the picky kids)

In a small pot over high heat, combine the blueberries and juice—and bring to a boil. Turn the heat down and simmer for 5 to 10 minutes, until the mixture becomes syrup-like.

Remove the sauce from the heat and pour into a blender or food processor. Blend until the sauce is jam-like. Store leftovers in an airtight container in the refrigerator.

BANANA BUTTER

One morning Jane was loving her banana bread muffin, but wanted to love it more. It just screamed for a pat of something, something moist and flavor enhancing. So she added a pat of banana—and Banana Butter was born!

Makes 8 to 10 pats

1 banana

Peel a banana, place it on a small plate, butter dish, or its own skin. Slice off a pat of banana (as you would a pat of butter) and spread on your Badass Banana Bread (page 254), Labor Day Zucchini Bread (page 255), Kale Blueberry Muffins (page 47) or anything that needs a sweet kiss of extra flavor.

RIP,

I appreciate the frankness with which you discuss health and diet...and the fact that you are in an "excitement-based" job like me.

    I'm an F-16 pilot stationed in Florida. Over the years I've put on a few pounds (especially after getting married) but haven't noticed trouble "pulling G's" or getting the job done. I have, however, been more and more sluggish—despite training for half-marathons, marathons, and working out. I just never felt I could get back to feeling great. Anyway, the Engine 2, whole-food plant-based diet (WFPBD as my wife and I call it) has given me a new surge of energy both mentally and physically. I feel much more ready to go fly a mission than I did previously. I've lost about 8 pounds and look to lose about 10 more to be back at my most fit weight.

    I've definitely kept the WFPBD a little quiet around the squadron—as most fighter pilots are die-hard meat eaters. But, I'll probably open up a bit more once I have some visible performance to back it up.

    Good luck with everything and thanks for the work.

—ED

LABOR DAY ZUCCHINI BREAD
(page 255)

BADASS BANANA BREAD
(page 254)

CHAPTER 5

APPETIZERS AND SIDES

TEXAS ARMADILLO TATER TOTS

These little taters carry big flavor and fun—and are as cute as a Texas armadillo! Dip the tots in ketchup (no high-fructose corn syrup) if that is your thing, or try Rip's Favorite Ranch (page 99).

Makes 18 tots

---

18 red baby potatoes, also called B size potatoes (close to the size of walnuts)

1 cup (8 ounces) Homemade Hummus (page 67) or store-bought hummus with no added oil or tahini

½ to ¾ cup water

2 tablespoons any Cajun seasoning (we prefer McCormick Perfect Pinch Cajun Seasoning; use more if you like it spicy and less if you don't like too much spice)

Preheat the oven to 425°F. Line a baking sheet with parchment paper.

Prepare the potatoes: Place a potato in the hollow of a wooden spoon, then make slices every ¼ inch going *nearly* the whole way down through the potato—so it looks like the work of an egg slicer.

In a food processor, combine the hummus, water, and 1 tablespoon of the seasoning and blend well. Place the mixture in a bowl.

Place the potatoes in the bowl and stir to coat with the mixture. Try to open the slices slightly to allow the coating to sneak all the way through. Place the coated potatoes on the lined pan. Sprinkle with the remaining seasoning.

Bake until the potatoes are cooked thoroughly, 45 minutes or longer (cooking time varies depending on the size of the potatoes). They should be tender in the center and crispy on the outside.

KICKIN' CORN MUFFINS

These sidekick muffins also make a hoppin' good corn bread. Corn flour is key to the recipe, yet it is sometimes difficult to find. To make your own corn flour, simply grind cornmeal in a high-speed blender until it becomes flour. Such a nifty, thrifty trick!

Makes 12 muffins

1 cup water

3 tablespoons flaxseed meal

1 ¼ cups oat flour

1 ¼ cups corn flour

½ teaspoon baking soda

½ cup 100% pure maple syrup

Preheat the oven to 350°F.

Combine the water and flaxseed meal in a small bowl and let sit for at least 5 minutes, until it starts to gel. (This is not the usual water-to-flaxseed-meal ratio used in baking: We are saving steps by using all the water for the muffins with the flaxseed meal.)

In a mixing bowl, combine the oat flour, corn flour, and baking soda. Add the flax mixture and maple syrup and mix until well combined.

Scoop the batter into the cups of a 12-cup nonstick muffin pan. Bake for 18 minutes, until lightly browned. These are best when served warm with salsa or hot sauce.

FIRE-ROASTED CORN

Our great-grandparents started the family fire-roasted corn tradition by grilling corn and spareribs over a huge open fire pit with a grill over the top. We ditched the spareribs over thirty years ago, but to this day we can't get enough of the fire-roasted corn.

Serves 6 to 12

EQUIPMENT

1 bucket filled with water

1 fire pit (or your backyard grill)

6 to 12 ears of corn, with husks intact

Soak the corn in the bucket of water for 1 to 5 minutes (or however long it takes you to get the fire going).

Start a fire in your fire pit (or grill). When the flames are low and the coals are hot, put the grill across the fire pit.

Place the soaked corn on the grill over the hot coals. Grill, turning the corn a quarter- or half-turn every 5 minutes. Be careful not to let the husks get dry and burn all the way through to the corn. The corn is ready when the kernels have self-steamed enough that they are a darker solid yellow color (not so with white corn!), about 20 minutes total. As you peel the husks backward, be careful, as they are hot. The cornhusks create a handle to hold the corn.

Hi, my name is Patrick and I'm a thirty-two-year-old firefighter/paramedic in Sarasota, Florida. I always battled with my weight and after graduating high school, it really piled on. I ate the typical "American diet" and would try to work out a couple of times a week, with no positive results. In fact, my favorite places to eat were the "all you can eat" buffets in town. My goal was to go in and eat so much that I would close them down…never happened! In June of 2011, I tore my ACL while on duty for the fire department. I had to have reconstructive knee surgery and was assigned to a desk for 10 months during my rehab.

I came across the *Forks over Knives* documentary and saw Rip climbing the fire pole without using his legs saying, "Real. Men. Eat. Plants!" and my eyes were opened! I began reading *The Engine 2 Diet* book and immediately switched to a plant-strong diet. I wasn't able to work out or do cardio during my rehab, but I wasn't going to allow that to stop my goals of losing weight and being healthy. I was so ignorant when I started eating this way that not only could I not pronounce quinoa correctly (*keeenowa*), I thought bok choy was a grain and was located in the grocery aisles! Jeez!

I'm 5 feet, 7 inches tall and when I started this journey, I weighed 255 pounds. I was wearing 44-inch-waist pants and thought that a 34-inch waist would be great for my height and body type. While assigned to my desk job for the ten months, I was able to lose 111 pounds and went down to a 30-inch waist! Since 2012 I have maintained my weight loss and am currently wearing 32-inch pants. Switching to a plant-strong lifestyle has changed my life in so many ways, and I've never felt better!

The one thing I want everyone to realize is you absolutely can accomplish what you put your mind to! Find something that motivates YOU and will keep you focused. For me, it was to one day wear a pair of 34-inch jeans from a store I could never shop at before. I purchased the exact size and style I wanted to wear, folded them up, and placed them next to my bed on my nightstand. They were the first thing I'd see when I woke up, and were the last thing I'd see before I went to bed. I didn't know how long it would take, but I truly believed I'd wear them one day. I was able to wear those jeans after nine months, and then they were too big! Believe in yourself, and use any negativity from others as fuel for your fire.

I am now the proud father of a beautiful little girl and I can't wait to watch her grow up living this healthy lifestyle. She will have the knowledge and tools to do this, thanks to Rip and his wonderful family.

—PATRICK DONOVAN, FIREFIGHTER

SIZZLIN' BABY BELLAS

Mushrooms are meaty! These baby bella mushrooms are sure to transform your brown rice from boring to bravo! Don't be surprised when the mushrooms sizzle, squeak, and squeal at you while cooking! Serve warm over brown rice, or cold alongside a hearty salad.

Makes about 3 cups

24 ounces whole baby bella mushrooms

1 to 3 tablespoons water

1 to 2 tablespoons low-sodium tamari

1 to 2 tablespoons balsamic vinegar

½ teaspoon dried oregano

½ teaspoon crushed rosemary

¼ teaspoon dried marjoram

2 cloves garlic, minced

Place a large skillet over high heat. When hot, add the mushrooms, stirring frequently. As they rub against the bottom of the hot pan they squeak and squeal! When they start to brown and lose a little of their fluid, decrease the heat to medium-high. Add 1 tablespoon water and cover. Stir intermittently at 1-minute intervals or so, replacing the lid after each stirring and adding 1 or 2 more tablespoons water as needed, for about 5 to 7 minutes. Taste a mushroom to make sure it is cooked completely. Remove from the heat and set aside.

In a medium bowl, combine the tamari, vinegar, oregano, rosemary, marjoram, and garlic. Add the mushrooms to the bowl and toss until well coated.

"KALE YEAH!" KALE CHIPS

These kale chips rarely make it off of the pan and into a bowl before they get eaten. They are that crispy and delicious. Yes, kale chips are all that—not the greasy, oily variety you find at the grocery store. These are the real deal!

Makes 2 to 3 baking sheets of kale chips, 8 to 10 servings

2 bunches kale, curly kale works best

½ cup cashews

¾ cup water

2 tablespoons taco seasoning (we prefer Ortega Taco Seasoning Mix with 40 percent less sodium)

½ cup nutritional yeast

Preheat the oven to 250°F. (Some ovens don't go as low as 250°F; just set it as low as it can go.) Line 2 or 3 baking sheets with parchment paper.

Strip the leaves from the ribs of the kale, and tear the leaves into 2- to 3-inch pieces.

In a food processor or high-speed blender, blend the cashews, water, taco seasoning, and nutritional yeast until it is a smooth sauce—like a slurry. Transfer the sauce to a large bowl, add the stripped kale leaves, and toss until well coated. Spread the coated kale leaves on the lined pans.

Bake for 2 hours or more. (Yeah, it takes a long time; if you bake in a convection oven, the chips will cook faster, around 40 minutes.) Keep checking on the chips to make sure they are drying out and not burning. As the kale shrinks, peek occasionally to make sure there are no clumps or layers sticking together. If so separate them—the kale needs to be one layer thick in order to get dried out and crispy like chips. Allow to cool before inhaling!

BEER BISCUITS

When Jane's kids first tried beer biscuits, they asked if they would get drunk! (We're not sure, but you probably don't want to make these at the fire station.) The key to the biscuits rising properly is to handle them gently and stir as little as possible. Warm from the oven, the biscuits go well with soups and salads, or dunked into True Grit Gravy (page 79).

Makes 8 to 10 biscuits

⅔ **cup walnuts**

2 **tablespoons water**

2 **cups white whole wheat flour, plus 1 tablespoon for dusting the board**

2 **tablespoons flaxseed meal**

½ **teaspoon baking soda**

½ **teaspoon baking powder**

¼ **teaspoon salt (optional)**

½ **cup beer, your favorite brand**

½ **cup oat milk**

Preheat the oven to 400°F. Line a baking sheet with parchment paper.

In a food processor, pulse the walnuts and water until a paste forms. Remove the walnut paste from the food processor (no need to clean it yet), and set aside.

In the food processor, combine the flour, flaxseed meal, baking soda, baking powder, and salt if using. Crumble the walnut paste on top of the flour in the food processor and carefully pulse the mixture 8 to 10 times, until everything mixes into a crumble with a mealy texture.

Transfer the mixture to a bowl. Pour in the beer and milk and gently mix and fold in all the ingredients until the flour is incorporated. Be careful not to overmix the dough.

Place the dough on a floured surface and gently press with your fingertips until roughly ½ inch thick. Use a drinking glass or biscuit cutter, cut out biscuits and place on the parchment-lined pan. Bake for 11 to 12 minutes, until lightly browned on top.

SEEDED RYE CRISPS

Who would ever make homemade crackers? You will! These easy-to-make seeded crispy crackers will amaze you and your guests. Dip them into your favorite homemade salsa (perhaps Brando Mango Salsa, page 86), or your favorite hummus or spread. We also love them with Beet Butter (page 61), Kale Butter 3.0 (page 58), and SoCo Guacamole (page 71).

TIP: If you like the taste, try adding some fennel seeds, too!

Makes 24 servings

1 ¼ cups old-fashioned oats

1 ¼ cups rye flour

1 cup flaxseeds

⅔ cup sesame seeds

⅓ cup poppy seeds

¼ teaspoon salt

2 cups water

Preheat the oven to 350°F. Line 2 large baking sheets with parchment paper.

In a food processor or high-speed blender, mix and crush the oats until they are coarsely chopped (do not make them into a fine flour).

In a mixing bowl, combine the oats, rye flour, flaxseeds, sesame seeds, poppy seeds, salt, and water. Let sit for 15 minutes to allow the water to be absorbed.

Spread the mix evenly and as thin as possible on the lined pans. For best results, try to flatten the mixture to less than ¼ inch. Bake for 15 minutes. Remove the trays from the oven and cut the mixture into desired cracker sizes with a pizza cutter or knife.

Return to the oven and bake for 40 minutes longer. Turn off the oven, open the oven door, and leave the crackers in the oven for 10 minutes. Close the oven door and let sit for 10 minutes longer. The crackers should be crisp. If they are not crispy, place back in the oven for 10 minutes at 350°F. Turn off the oven again, open the oven door, and let the crackers remain in the oven for 10 minutes, followed by 10 minutes with the door closed. Allow to cool and serve. Store in an airtight container for 2 weeks.

DECK GUN NACHOS

On top of fire engines there is a fixed deck gun. These deck guns can swivel 360 degrees and release massive amounts of water to overwhelm raging flames that rise 150 to 300 feet. These nachos will deliver by dousing your taste buds and your stomach with everything you need to satisfy your nacho cravings!

Makes 1 sheet pan–full

Corn Chips (page 132), equal to about 12 corn tortillas made into chips

1 to 2 cups fat-free vegetarian refried beans (we prefer Casa Fiesta brand)

2 tomatoes, chopped

1 to 2 tablespoons nutritional yeast

3 to 4 green onions, finely chopped

1 cup salsa, your favorite

1½ cups Roasted Corn Salsa (page 84)

SoCo Guacamole (page 71)

Preheat the oven to 350°F. Line a baking sheet with parchment paper.

Place half of the chips on the lined pan. (If the chips are not really crispy, first crisp them in the oven for 5 minutes.) Cover the chips with the refried beans. This is not a neat process; use a spoon and plop the beans onto the chips. Sprinkle the tomatoes and the nutritional yeast on top of the beans. Bake for 10 to 15 minutes, until the beans are warm throughout.

Remove the nachos from the oven and add the green onions, store-bought salsa, corn salsa, and guacamole and dig in with the remaining chips. Cheers!

SAVORY SCALLOPED POTATOES

Rip's wife, Jill, was lying in bed one night craving scalloped potatoes in gravy like the dish her mother made when she was growing up in Wisconsin. The next day she experimented with making a plant-strong version and totally nailed it!

Serves 6 to 8

8 to 10 Yukon Gold potatoes, cut in half and thinly sliced (about 7 cups)

½ onion, thinly sliced

2 cups low-sodium vegetable broth

2 tablespoons low-sodium tamari or Bragg Liquid Aminos

1 teaspoon garlic powder

½ teaspoon dried sage

½ teaspoon dried thyme

½ teaspoon black pepper

3 tablespoons whole wheat flour (or any thickening agent, such as corn starch)

Preheat the oven to 400°F.

Place the potatoes and onions in a 9x13-inch casserole dish.

In a small bowl, stir together the broth, tamari, garlic powder, sage, thyme, and black pepper and stir well. Whisk in the flour until there are no clumps. Pour the mixture over the potatoes and onions and, using a small fork, gently stir until all the potatoes are well doused.

Cover with a lid or aluminum foil and bake for 1 hour and 20 minutes, until the potatoes are soft and the liquid starts thickening. Uncover, stir, and continue to bake uncovered for 15 to 20 minutes, until the potatoes are browned.

BEST DAMN FRIES

The trick to these fries is cooking the potatoes in advance so they can cool overnight before you bake them into fries. This way the potatoes are already cooked through and through! Each individual fry has to be touching the surface of the parchment in order to get crispy and brown.

VARIATIONS: Try making small fries with small new potatoes and following the technique above. Or sweet potato fries with sweet potatoes instead of the Yukon Golds.

Serves 6 to 8

6 Yukon Gold potatoes

Ketchup (no high-fructose corn syrup), for serving

A day before, preheat the oven to 400°F. Bake the potatoes for 45 to 60 minutes, until cooked through. Let cool overnight in the refrigerator.

Preheat the oven to 400°F. Line a baking sheet with parchment paper.

Cut the potatoes into fries or wedges. Place on the parchment with each fry lying flat on the paper— be sure none are on top of another. Bake for 10 minutes. Turn each fry and bake for 10 minutes longer, until browned. Serve warm with ketchup.

BBQ EGGPLANT ROUNDS

These are easy to make, look crispy and delicious, and taste fabulous! Rip can't stand eggplant (it's something about the texture) but these are an exception to the rule. Try them in sandwiches— just cut them a wee bit thicker and you are off to the picnic. We like to use Bone Suckin' barbecue sauce or Robbie's Hickory sauce, but feel free to use the sauce of your choice.

Serves 2 to 6, depending on eggplant size

1 eggplant

¼ cup barbecue sauce

¼ cup nutritional yeast

1 tablespoon balsamic vinegar

Preheat the oven to 450°F. Line 2 baking sheets with parchment paper.

Slice the eggplant into about ¼-inch-thick slices, or as thin as you can make them. (We recommend leaving the skin on because it's good for you, but if you don't like it, peel it off.)

Place the slices on the parchment paper and spread a very thin layer of barbecue sauce on each with a spoon, then sprinkle with nutritional yeast. Flip the slices over, spread a thin layer of sauce on tops, sprinkle with nutritional yeast, and add a few drops of balsamic vinegar.

Bake, checking frequently so they don't burn, for 15 to 20 minutes, until browned. They are best when they are just on the edge of burning. Remove to a platter with a spatula. You will not believe how crispy they are or how good they taste.

ROASTED CAULIFLOWER STEAKS

If there's one vegetable that is a low-maintenance cool cat, it's cauliflower. It has the ability to transform itself into anything from rice to sauces to steaks! Enjoy these roasted cauliflower steaks as an appetizer or as part of the main course.

Serves 8 as an appetizer or side dish, or 2 as a main course

1 head cauliflower

2 tablespoons low-sodium tamari or Bragg Liquid Aminos

2 to 4 tablespoons nutritional yeast

Preheat the oven to 400°F and line a baking pan with parchment paper.

Core the head of cauliflower, then cut into long, flat slices. Place flat on the lined pan and drizzle all the slices with the tamari (or spray with Bragg's), followed by a sprinkle of nutritional yeast.

Bake for 25 to 30 minutes, until the cauliflower is well browned and even a little crispy.

The idea of becoming a plant-based eater for any reason was not possible! I had been a lover of copious amounts of meat, dairy, and refined grains for my whole lifetime. However, being a member of an at-risk group for many chronic diseases (African American), I found myself on the edge of a bottomless precipice ready to fall in at the very time the Seven-Day Rescue opportunity came along.

At the beginning of this program I was so worried about where I was going to get enough protein. Then I learned, "It's all in the plants and from my own body!" Think of the wildebeest, bison, elephant, giraffe, gazelle, zebra, horse, and the powerful gorilla, along with other numerous animals of the forest and field, that are exclusively plant-strong! When I saw this list my mind began to turn, slowly...

Therefore, I embraced the Engine 2 "Plant Strong" regimen of no salt, no added fat, including all oils, no sugar, no meat, no dairy, and no eggs!

I ate a vast variety of plant-strong meals filled with robust flavor and exciting spiciness and creamy decadence and I was never hungry!

—DAVID HONORÉ, BAKER

ROASTED RED BELL PEPPERS

Roasted peppers are what make the sandwich, the salad, the pizza, the pocket, the burrito...you get my drift. Make these, share these, and devour these. You will become addicted.

Makes 3 to 4 cups

6 red bell peppers

3 tablespoons balsamic vinegar

2 teaspoons minced garlic

1 teaspoon dried basil

1 teaspoon dried thyme

1 teaspoon dried rosemary

1 teaspoon dried marjoram

1 teaspoon dried oregano

Preheat the oven to 450°F or set to broil.

Place the peppers on a baking sheet and roast or broil until blackened on one side, about 5 to 7 minutes. Turn the peppers and continue roasting, rotating until all sides are blackened, about 5 to 7 minutes per side. Some people prefer roasting peppers individually over a gas flame which works, too.

Let cool slightly, then peel and seed the peppers under running water. Slice or tear the flesh into long strips and place in a bowl. Add the vinegar, garlic, basil, thyme, rosemary, marjoram, and oregano. Allow the peppers and spices to marinate for at least 30 minutes. Store in an airtight container for 7 days.

TACO SHELLS OR TOSTADOS

Some meals just need a vehicle to transport the delicious meal into your mouth—as in our Exploding Burritos (page 238). Happily, corn tortillas can be easily made into taco-shaped shells or tostados (flat, crispy tortillas).

Makes 10 taco shells or tostados

1 package corn tortillas, usually contains 10 tortillas

Preheat the oven to 350°F.

For taco shells, drape one tortilla over two slats of the oven rack, allowing the rounded sides to hang down. Repeat for as many taco shells as you desire.

For tostados, lay tortillas flat on the oven rack.

Bake for 8 to 10 minutes, checking occasionally as they may burn and oven temperatures vary. Remove from the oven when they are crisp. As they cool a bit, they get even crispier. Serve or store in airtight containers to keep crisp.

PITA CHIPS

It is hard to have a conversation while eating these chips as they are so crispy, crunchy, and loud.

Makes 36 pita chips

6 whole wheat pita bread rounds

Preheat the oven to 350°F. Slice the pita bread rounds into 6 triangular sections or strips. Bake for 8 minutes, until crisp.

CORN CHIPS OR RICE CHIPS

These crispy chips are great for any dip.

Yield varies with different shapes

Corn, rice, or whole wheat tortillas (or wraps)

Preheat the oven to 350°F. Slice the tortillas into sections or strips. Bake for 8 minutes, until crisp.

TORTILLA BOWLS

We love these fun, edible bowls. The forms to make them are available online and at Bed Bath & Beyond.

Makes 6 edible bowls

6 wheat, multigrain, corn, or rice tortillas

Preheat the oven to 350°F. Place tortillas in tortilla bowl forms. Bake for 8 minutes, until crisp and solid.

FRIDAYS

One of the many things Jane does in addition to lecturing, food demos, dancing, and keeping the energy high during our week-long immersion programs in Sedona, Arizona, is to lead the gorgeous morning walks. During the walks, she has some great open conversations with the participants. On one of these walks they started talking about going to the bathroom. All the participants started sharing how excited they were about how often they were visiting the toilet. After a short pause, one of the women remarked it had been four days and she still hadn't gone to the bathroom. There was an audible gasp from the group, and then the woman went on to mention how all her life she only went to the bathroom on Fridays. In fact, it was such a regular occurrence that long ago she had affectionately named her bowel movements "Fridays." Walking with Jane the next morning, she confided that she went to the bathroom—and that it wasn't on a Friday for the first time in as long as she could remember! Jane checked in with her "Friday" friend several weeks later to discover she was now going to the bathroom several times a week and that they were all smooth as Sunday morning. Time for a new name…

VOLLEYBALL BEAN SALAD
(page 146)

CHAPTER 6

SALADS AND CROUTONS

"KALE, CAESAR!" SALAD

The minute we met Sandy we fell for her great energy and endless generosity of spirit. A health scare got her on a plant-based diet, and she has not looked back for a moment! She teaches plant-based eating in Southern California—and she shared this winner of a recipe with us! We have fallen hard for it and you will, too!

Serves 6 to 8

1 large white onion, halved and thinly sliced into ¼-inch-thick half-moons

1 large head lacinato kale, stripped of ribs and chopped into thin strips

Sandy's Caesar Dressing (page 92)

1 large head romaine lettuce, chopped into thin strips

Homemade Croutons (page 152) or Sweet Potato Croutons (page 155)

Preheat the oven to 400°F. Line a baking sheet with parchment paper.

Place the sliced onions on the pan and bake for 30 minutes, until tender and fully cooked—but do not burn.

Place the kale strips in a large bowl. Add the still-warm onions and toss with the kale. This will cause the kale to become a bit more tender. Let cool.

Add 4 to 5 tablespoons dressing to the bowl and massage the dressing into the kale and onions—either with a wooden spoon or, ideally, your hands. Next toss in the romaine lettuce. There should be roughly equal amounts of romaine and kale. Add as many croutons as desired and more salad dressing until you get the desired consistency. Toss and serve immediately.

SMOKY WALNUT AND QUINOA SALAD

Ever been to a fancy bistro where they served a froufrou salad topped with candied walnuts? Well who knew those crunchy nuggets were loaded with butter and sugar? Now you can enjoy that fancy-schmancy bistro salad at home, but accented with plant-strong smoky walnuts.

Serves 4

2 cups quinoa

1 tablespoon 100% pure maple syrup

½ teaspoon smoked paprika

¼ teaspoon cinnamon

¼ teaspoon chipotle powder

Pinch of salt (optional)

Pinch of black pepper

1 cup walnuts

4 cups fresh arugula and spinach mix

2 to 3 green onions, chopped

1 cup cherry tomatoes, halved

⅓ cup dried cranberries

2 tablespoons capers

½ cup, or desired amount, dressing of choice (we suggest Ginger, Walnut, and Miso Dressing, page 100)

Preheat the oven or toaster oven to 350°F. Line a small pan with parchment paper. Prepare quinoa per package instructions.

In a small bowl, combine the maple syrup, paprika, cinnamon, chipotle powder, salt if using, and black pepper and stir until well combined. Add the walnuts and stir until well coated. Place the walnuts on the lined pan and toast in the oven or toaster oven for 10 minutes, until the coating is no longer wet but crisp and fragrant. Keep a close eye on the nuts as they burn easily.

In a salad bowl, combine the quinoa, arugula and spinach, green onions, tomatoes, cranberries, and capers. Toss the salad well then top with the walnuts and your favorite dressing.

MAGNETIC WILD RICE SALAD

Every year, Jane and her coven of girlfriends and their families gather together for a magical visit at our family farm. There are twenty-two altogether, so they divide up the meal duties among the five families. One of the coven members, Magnetic Pennie, a bright-eyed Dane who draws everyone into her beautiful, colorful world, makes this fresh, colorful wild rice salad for lunch each year. It is a universal hit. Don't know what to make for your next gathering? This is the ticket.

Serves 6

2 cups cooked wild rice

4 stalks celery, chopped

½ bunch parsley, stemmed and chopped

4 green onions, chopped

1 Granny Smith apple, cubed

1 cup mandarin oranges, drained

½ cup dried cranberries

¼ cup walnuts, in pieces

1 avocado, cubed (optional)

6 tablespoons red wine vinegar, or more to taste

Prepare the wild rice as directed on package; this is usually 3:1 water to wild rice ratio. Let cool.

In a beautiful salad bowl, toss together the wild rice, celery, parsley, green onions, apple, oranges, cranberries, walnuts, avocado if using, and vinegar. Taste to see if you prefer more red wine vinegar. It is up to your preference! Serve at room temperature or chilled.

WATERMELON TABBOULEH SALAD

This is an ideal salad when it's way too hot outside and even the thought of turning on the stove makes you sweat.

Serves 6

1 cup uncooked bulgur wheat

2 cups water

2 cups fresh parsley, finely chopped

¼ cup fresh mint, finely chopped

4 green onions, finely chopped

2 tomatoes, diced

2 cups (or more) watermelon balls (cubes are fine if you do not have a melon baller), plus additional 1 cup watermelon pieces

1 medium cucumber, seeded and diced

¼ teaspoon ground cumin

3 tablespoons fresh lemon juice

Prepare the bulgur: The ratio is similar to rice, but it takes less time to cook. In a pot with a lid, bring the bulgur and water to a boil; cover and simmer for 12 to 15 minutes, until tender. Drain off any excess liquid and set aside. Let cool.

In a medium bowl, toss together the parsley, mint, green onions, tomatoes, watermelon balls, cucumber, cumin, and lemon juice. Add the cooled bulgur and toss until it looks like a well-mixed tabbouleh salad.

In a small blender or a food processor, blend the 1 cup watermelon pieces until liquefied. Pour the watermelon juice over the tabbouleh. (This is the secret ingredient that, according to Brian, adds delicious moisture and sweetness, especially since we don't use oil!)

CHATELAINE SALAD

The inspiration for this salad was in a Canadian magazine called *Chatelaine*—the equivalent of *Better Homes and Gardens* meets *Cosmopolitan*. The variety of ingredients and textures is wildly exciting: jicama, avocado, radishes, toasted pumpkin seeds (pepitas), mint, and orange segments for starters. Enjoy the salad no matter which side of the border you live on!

Serves 2 to 3

Grated zest of 1 lime

Juice of 1 lime (about 2 tablespoons)

2 teaspoons orange juice

2 teaspoons Dijon mustard

2 teaspoons 100% pure maple syrup

½ teaspoon chili powder

1 orange, peeled and divided into segments (segments halved if you prefer)

1 medium jicama, peeled and cubed

1 avocado, cubed

4 radishes, thinly sliced

⅓ cup Toasted Pepitas (page 152)

¼ cup finely diced red onion

2 tablespoons coarsely chopped mint

In a large bowl, whisk the lime zest and juice, orange juice, mustard, maple syrup, and chili powder until well mixed. Toss in the orange segments, jicama, avocado, and radishes until well coated. Top with the pepitas, red onion, and mint and serve.

CHICK & SALAD

Say it fast and crazily, and it sounds like *chick-en salad.* And amazingly, it *tastes* like chicken salad! Chick & Salad makes great sandwiches, too. Once Jane was hosting a dinner for about 11 people and she did not know what to serve! So as usual she went overboard and made way too much food. But guess what the favorite dish was for everyone at the table? Chick & Salad! We love repeating and repeating the name: "Chick & Salad!" Serve on a bed of lettuce, on toast, in a sandwich, or right out of the bowl!

Serves 4

1 cup finely chopped green cabbage or Napa cabbage

½ medium sweet onion, finely diced (about 1 cup)

2 long celery stalks, finely chopped

½ cup shredded carrots

¼ cup raisins

5 dried apricots, finely chopped

1 (15-ounce) can chickpeas, drained and rinsed

1 cup Homemade Hummus (page 67) or store-bought hummus with no added oil or tahini

Pinch cayenne pepper (optional)

1 squirt sriracha or hot sauce of your choice

In a bowl, combine all the ingredients and stir together until everything is coated.

VOLLEYBALL BEAN SALAD

Men's Health magazine gets a nod for this salad: We read about it in an interview with Dustin Watten, an awesome American volleyball player. It is packed with color, power, and flavor. We had to change a few ingredients to suit our plant-strong guidelines, but we do that a lot. And please don't be afraid of recipes that look good even if they are not plant-strong: You can always skip the added oil, use nondairy milk, and try spices instead of all the added salt.

Serves 2 to 4

1 (15-ounce) can red kidney beans, drained and rinsed

½ red bell pepper, julienned

2 green onions, finely chopped

3 tablespoons finely diced red onion

1 tablespoon finely minced seeded jalapeño pepper, or to taste

¼ cup fresh cilantro, coarsely chopped

1 to 2 tablespoons red wine vinegar, to taste

Black pepper, to taste

1 to 2 tablespoons Toasted Pepitas (page 152)

1 cup, or desired amount, dressing of choice (we recommend Mango Lemon Dressing, page 97)

In a salad bowl, mix the kidney beans, bell pepper, green onions, red onion, jalapeño, and cilantro. Add the vinegar and dash of pepper, toss, and top with the pepitas. Add your plant-strong dressing of choice and toss.

KALE CRUNCH SALAD

Cooked kale and Brussels sprouts are a sure thing in our home, but this salad surprised all of us. The raw ingredients are finely shaved, chopped, or matchsticked, creating a crunchy delight. If Texans are around, we serve it with Sweet Fire Dressing (page 101); if not, we prefer Eternal Dressing (page 96) or Rip's Favorite Ranch (page 99).

Serves 4 or more

2 cups kale, stripped of ribs and finely chopped

1 cup raw Brussels sprouts, thinly sliced (almost shaved)

1 cup matchstick carrots

1 head broccoli, thinly sliced (almost shaved)

¼ green cabbage, finely chopped

¼ purple cabbage, finely chopped

1 cup or desired amount, dressing of choice

In a large salad bowl, combine the kale, Brussels sprouts, carrots, broccoli, green cabbage, and purple cabbage. Toss with your favorite dressing.

I read your book *The Engine 2 Diet* and when I came to the part that type 2 diabetes was an easy fix, my husband's ears pricked up and he said, "What? Read that again!" And I did. He became so excited. He hated being a diabetic. "Let's do the diet!" said he. So we did. Eight months later Dean has dropped 80 pounds and today his blood work came back normal. His A1C was 5.3!

"Good work," said his doctor. "Good work," says me. We are plant-strong for life now...thanks to you and your dad. *Forks over Knives* was a big eye-opener and we appreciated all the work your family has done for us. I have all your cookbooks and your sister Jane's also...and I am quite the good cook now. I dropped 40 pounds also and my cholesterol with it. You are such a pioneer and I am so thankful we had the smarts to realize it.

—MELODY STARMER

BAJA SLAW

Baja Slaw. Baja Slaw. We cannot say it enough to emphasize the zest and heat this fiery dish ignites. Warning: It is not the prettiest dish, but it wins you over with flavor. We suggest you serve it in various ways: as a salad dressing, on top of rice and beans, as a burger dip, or as a chip dip.

Serves 4 to 6

1 ripe avocado, pitted and peeled

1¼ cups salsa, your choice (we prefer tomatillo-based)

1 teaspoon fresh lemon juice

1 clove garlic, finely minced

Pinch cayenne, if you like it hot

1 to 3 shakes red pepper flakes, depending on your heat tolerance

4 to 6 cups finely shredded red or green cabbage (we like to use both colors)

½ cup shredded carrots

½ red bell pepper, diced

1 tomato, diced

Fresh cilantro, chopped, for garnish (optional)

In a food processor or high-speed blender, combine the avocado, salsa, lemon juice, garlic, cayenne, and red pepper flakes and blend until smooth to make the Baja sauce.

In a bowl, combine the cabbage and sauce, and toss until everything is well coated. Add the carrots, bell pepper, and tomato and toss again. Garnish with cilantro and serve immediately or place in the fridge until ready to serve.

SIDE CAR SALAD

Our Side Car Salad is one zippy dish. The zip and zap of the arugula, radishes, and wasabi will keep you humming along! It is just perfect to ride alongside a plant-strong burger! The wasabi can be cut in half if the heat is too much for you.

Serves 4

2 teaspoons wasabi powder (or more if you dare!)

¼ cup water

1 teaspoon rice vinegar

2 cups arugula

1 cup thinly sliced radishes

2 medium cucumbers or 1 long English cucumber, thinly sliced

4 sprigs fresh dill, chopped

Black pepper to taste

In a small bowl, combine the wasabi powder and water and mix until smooth. Stir in the vinegar.

In a bowl, combine the arugula, radishes, and cucumbers. Pour the wasabi mixture over the vegetables and add the dill. Toss together and chill for 1 hour before serving. Top with fresh ground pepper.

TOASTED PEPITAS (PUMPKIN SEEDS)

Toasted pumpkin seeds add a satisfying crunch and nutty flavor to most everything. Use as a topping for salads, or in sandwiches—anywhere that needs a tasty little crunch.

Makes ½ cup

½ cup pumpkin seeds, raw and unsalted

Preheat the oven to 350°F and line a baking pan with parchment paper, or heat a skillet over medium heat.

Spread the seeds in the baking pan or skillet so there is only a single layer. Bake in the oven for 12 to 15 minutes, or toast in the skillet for 6 to 8 minutes, until browned and crisp.

HOMEMADE CROUTONS

When our kids started eating salads with us they always had to have croutons on top. If there were no croutons, there was no salad eating. So we would grab any bread product within reach, chop it into cubes, and throw them in the oven! Anything to get them to like salad!

TIP: Add seasonings before toasting, if you prefer.

Makes 1½ to 2 cups

1 chunk stale or fresh 100% whole-grain bread, or a whole wheat bagel

Preheat the oven or toaster oven to 325°F.

Cut the bread or bagel into cubes. Arrange on a pan and bake for 15 to 20 minutes. If the croutons are not crispy, continue baking for 3 to 4 minutes longer. Remove and let cool before tossing on a salad.

HOMEMADE CROUTONS
(opposite)

TOASTED PEPITAS
(opposite)

SWEET POTATO CROUTONS
(page 155)

HOT CHICKPEA CROUTONS
(page 154)

HOT CHICKPEA CROUTONS

These crispy little numbers make a great snack, addition to a salad, or topping for a one-bowl meal.

JANE'S TIP: "Sometimes I turn the oven off after 30 minutes and leave them to crisp up while I drive carpool. Then they get really crispy!"

Makes about 1 cup

1 (15-ounce) can chickpeas

½ teaspoon onion powder

¼ teaspoon garlic salt (or ¼ teaspoon garlic powder and ¼ teaspoon salt)

¼ teaspoon ground cumin

¼ teaspoon chili powder

Pinch cayenne pepper

Pinch white pepper

Preheat the oven to 400°F. Line a baking pan with parchment paper.

In a colander, drain and rinse the chickpeas. You'll see that the chickpeas have skins like little clear jackets around each. Rub the chickpeas a little bit so that the skins loosen, then remove as many as you can.

Still in the colander, add the onion powder, garlic salt, cumin, chili powder, cayenne, and white pepper and toss.

Pour the coated chickpeas onto the parchment-lined pan and bake for 30 to 40 minutes—until crisp, crisp, crisp!

SWEET POTATO CROUTONS

These croutons are delicious just for snacking. It was hard to place them in the crouton section and not just in their own *Snack on Me* section. But in the spirit of their shape we call them croutons, not in the spirit of their dry crunch. They add a boom of flavor to your salad and more than a snap of crisp.

Makes 1½ to 2 cups

1 large sweet potato, unpeeled

1 tablespoon Mrs. Dash seasoning blend, or your favorite seasoning—like a no-salt Cajun seasoning

1 tablespoon flaxseed meal

Preheat the oven to 400°F. Line a baking sheet with parchment paper.

Cook the sweet potato in whatever way works best for you until soft throughout: Bake in a 400°F oven for 45 minutes, or cook in the microwave for 8 minutes. Peel the sweet potato.

Cut the cooked sweet potato into cubes. Try to make them uniform in size so they bake evenly. Rinse the cubes with water and place in a bowl.

Sprinkle the seasoning and flaxseed meal over the cubes and toss until well coated.

Place on the lined pan and bake for 20 minutes, or until browned a bit. Cool and add to salads just like croutons!

SOUL-WARMING TOMATO SOUP
(page 167)

CHAPTER 7

SOUPS AND SANDWICHES

PIERCE'S RED LENTIL SOUP

One of our favorite people in the whole world is the effervescent and dynamic Cindy Pierce. Cindy has written three books on sex, and travels around the country speaking about this tricky topic with students, parents, and educators—somehow with humor. She grew up in Hanover, New Hampshire, at her parents' B and B, Pierce's Inn. We feast on the inn's home-brewed red lentil creation whenever we visit. It is a beautiful orange-red—like a New England fall day—and as dynamic as Cindy herself. Serve with Kickin' Corn Muffins (page 111) or over brown rice, quinoa, or alone.

Serves 6

1 large onion, diced

5 carrots, chopped

5 celery stalks, chopped

1 glove garlic, minced

1 teaspoon turmeric

1 teaspoon ground coriander

½ teaspoon ground cumin

½ teaspoon chili powder

1 cup red lentils

5 cups low-sodium vegetable broth

1 bay leaf

Pinch of salt (optional)

Black pepper, to taste

In a deep pot over medium-high heat, cook the onion, carrots, and celery, stirring until soft, 18 to 20 minutes.

In a small bowl, combine the garlic, turmeric, coriander, cumin, and chili powder. Add the spice mixture to the pot and stir well, until all the vegetables are well coated with spices.

Add the lentils, cover with all the broth, and toss in the bay leaf. Bring to a boil, then reduce the heat and simmer for 10 minutes, or until the lentils are soft. Remove the bay leaf. Season with salt and pepper.

Using an immersion blender or food processor, blend the soup until smooth in texture, or to your liking. This soup is great to freeze and serve later.

KICKIN' CORN MUFFINS
(page 111)

SWEET POTATO AND SHIITAKE SOUP

This soup is delicious and filling. Serve for lunch or over brown rice or quinoa for a heartier dinner. Any sweet potatoes are good but Yellow Jersey sweet potatoes (which are white) are especially sweet and delicious! The more fresh basil, the better, so pile it on if you choose. The same is true of spinach: It's hard to get too much. Serve the soup with a huge green salad or pile of cooked greens.

TIP: You can also reconstitute 1 cup dried shiitakes and use instead of the 4 ounces fresh. Simply soak them in warm water for 30 minutes, drain, and discard any stems before slicing.

Serves 4 to 6

1 large leek, white and green parts, chopped

8 cloves garlic, minced

4 ounces fresh shiitake mushrooms, sliced (about 2 cups)

1 large bay leaf

6 cups low-sodium vegetable broth

1½ cups red lentils

1 large sweet potato, scrubbed and cut into ½-inch cubes

5 ounces fresh spinach, or more to taste

1 cup fresh basil, chopped

1 tablespoon balsamic vinegar

2 pinches ground cayenne pepper, or to taste

Black pepper, to taste

Sprinkle of Mrs. Dash garlic and herb seasoning mix, or other salt-free spice mix of your choice

In a large soup pot over medium-high heat, cook the leek, garlic, mushrooms, and bay leaf for 5 to 8 minutes, until the leek has softened. Add splashes of broth or water if the leek is sticking. Stir in the broth, lentils, and sweet potato and bring to a boil. Lower the heat, cover, and simmer for 30 to 40 minutes, until the lentils and sweet potato are soft, but not mushy.

Remove the bay leaf. With an immersion blender, purée the soup until it is partially smooth. If you do not have an immersion blender, remove 2 cups soup and purée in a food processor or blender. Return the purée to the pot and stir into the soup.

Add the spinach, basil, vinegar, cayenne, and black pepper and cook a minute more, until the spinach softens. Serve with a garnishing sprinkle of Mrs. Dash.

YUMMY YAM AND YELLOW PEA SOUP

Yams + Yellow peas = Yum. If yellow peas are not easily available, green split peas will also work. In case the whole yam thing is throwing you, here's the deal: Yams are not related to sweet potatoes although their appearance and flavor are similar. Yams have a much thicker skin and can grow to be six feet in length and weigh up to 120 pounds! But for the purposes of this soup, either yams (a smaller version) or sweet potatoes will do. Serve along with a huge green salad or pile of cooked greens.

TIP: Try Japanese sweet potatoes; they are amazingly sweet!

Serves 6 to 8

1 large onion, diced

2 tablespoons minced fresh ginger

3 cloves garlic, minced

2 tablespoons curry powder

1 teaspoon ground cumin

½ teaspoon dry mustard

½ teaspoon ground turmeric

⅛ teaspoon cayenne pepper

1 large yam or Japanese sweet potato, cut into 1-inch cubes

3 large carrots, chopped

8 cups low-sodium vegetable broth

2 cups dried yellow split peas (we recommend Goya brand; avoid bulk yellow split peas as they may not soften when cooked)

1 bunch kale (or any leafy greens like collards or Swiss chard), stripped of ribs and chopped into bite-size pieces

Black pepper, to taste

In a large soup pot over medium-high heat, cook the onion, stirring, until translucent, about 5 minutes. Add the ginger and garlic and cook for 5 more minutes. Pour a tablespoon or more of water in the pot to prevent sticking, if necessary.

Add the curry, cumin, mustard, turmeric, cayenne, yam, carrots, broth, and split peas to the pot. Bring to a boil, cover, and simmer until the split peas are tender, broken down, and sort of creamy, 60 to 90 minutes. Stir occasionally to make sure the peas don't stick to the bottom of the pot.

About 10 minutes before the soup is done, add the chopped kale, stir, and cook for about 10 minutes, until they soften and integrate with the rest of the soup. Add freshly ground pepper to taste and more broth or water if too thick for your liking.

SNAPPY BLACK BEAN SOUP

This easy bean soup is ideal for a lunch meeting or a cozy family dinner. The black beans and lentils provide heartiness and the salsa, orange juice, and spices ratchet up the flavor. Serve with Brando Mango Salsa (page 86) on top.

TIP: To make 1½ cups cooked lentils from dry lentils: Bring 3 cups water to a boil, add 1 cup dry lentils, and simmer until soft, about 20 minutes. Pour off any excess water.

Serves 4 to 6

3 (15-ounce) cans no-salt black beans, drained and rinsed

1 (15-ounce) can lentils, drained and rinsed, or 1½ cups cooked lentils (see Tip above)

1 cup salsa, your favorite

Juice of ½ orange (2 to 3 tablespoons)

1 clove garlic, minced

1 teaspoon ground cumin

¼ teaspoon garlic salt or garlic powder

1½ to 2 cups low-sodium vegetable broth or water, to reach desired consistency

1 to 2 green onions, chopped, for garnish

In a medium pot over medium-high heat, combine the beans, lentils, salsa, orange juice, garlic, cumin, garlic salt, and broth. Once heated up, use an immersion blender to liquefy the soup. Or throw the contents of the pot into a food processor or high-speed blender to blend the mixture. Serve warm with a garnish of green onions.

Following your Engine 2 diet has changed my life! I have lost over 80 pounds and never felt better. Although I take a lot of criticism from friends, I know that living a plant-strong lifestyle is the best choice that I have ever made. The health benefits, helping to reduce environmental devastation, and having compassion for all living things is something that I am proud of and will never ever change in my life! I am excited to try out the recipes in your new book!

—CHERI HARDT, BARTENDER

TIME TRAVELER PARSNIP SOUP

One of Jane's favorite novel series, *Outlander,* has to do with time travel. She can sit on the couch reading and eating this soup into the wee hours of the night and be fully transported to the Jacobite Rising of 1745. Serve with a scoop of brown rice and a sprinkling of freshly ground black pepper alongside a huge salad!

Serves 4

1 cup dry lentils, or 1 (15-ounce) can lentils, drained and rinsed

1 large onion, diced

2 cloves garlic, minced

½- to 1-inch piece fresh ginger, peeled and finely chopped (more ginger creates more heat and bite)

¼ teaspoon ground cardamom

¼ teaspoon ground cumin

¼ teaspoon cayenne pepper

1 pound parsnips (like carrots, they vary in size, so weigh them at the store), peeled and cut into ½-inch cubes

3½ cups low-sodium vegetable broth

1 cup oat milk

Black pepper, to taste

If using uncooked dry lentils: Bring 3 cups water to a boil, add the lentils, and simmer until soft, about 20 minutes. Drain any extra water off and set aside.

In a pot over high heat, cook the onion, stirring occasionally, for about 5 minutes, until soft and browned a bit. Turn the heat down to medium, add the garlic, ginger, cardamom, cumin, cayenne, and parsnips and stir until everything is well coated with spices. Add the broth and milk and simmer for 20 minutes, or until the parsnips are soft. Add the cooked or canned lentils and continue cooking for 5 more minutes.

Using an immersion blender right in the pot, or a food processor or high-speed blender, purée the soup until smooth, or to the texture of your liking. Add black pepper to taste.

SOUL-WARMING TOMATO SOUP

When Jane was visiting with her coven of girlfriends, her pal Elizabeth showed up with a cauldron of this beautiful tomato soup. They sat around all afternoon chatting and dipping bread into the soul-warming soup.

Serves 4

1 medium onion, chopped

3 to 5 cloves garlic, minced

1 large bay leaf

2 (28-ounce) cans crushed tomatoes

1 tablespoon 100% pure maple syrup

3 slices 100% whole-grain bread, torn into 1-inch pieces

2 cups low-sodium vegetable broth

¼ teaspoon white pepper

¼ teaspoon crushed black pepper, or to taste

Chopped fresh parsley, for garnish

100% whole-grain bread, for serving

In a soup pot over medium-high heat, cook the onion, garlic, and bay leaf for about 5 minutes, until soft and translucent. Turn the heat to high and add the tomatoes with their juice, the maple syrup, bread pieces, and broth. Add the white pepper and black pepper, bring to a boil, and then turn to low and simmer for 5 minutes more. The bread will be saturated and dissolving into the soup. Remove the bay leaf.

With an immersion blender, or in a food processor or high-speed blender, blend to the texture you prefer. Some like it smooth and others like it with texture; it is up to you. Garnish with parsley and serve with thick hunks of whole-grain bread and enjoy all afternoon with your pals.

BLT&A

Jane asked her kids if they were fired up for the BLTs for dinner—curious if her plant-strong kids even knew what *BLT* means. Their response: "Well, what will our 'B' be since we don't eat bacon?" Ha! **B**aked tofu, **L**ettuce, **T**omato, and **A**vocado. They devoured the sandwiches!

The key is to soak the tofu in the marinade for at least an hour.

Makes 4 sandwiches

1 pound firm tofu, extra-firm tofu, or tempeh

Smoky Bake-On Marinade (page 80)

8 slices 100% whole-grain bread (we prefer Alvarado St. Bakery no-salt-added sprouted multi-grain bread)

1 large or 2 small avocados: ½ thinly sliced, ½ smashed to be used as a spread

4 ounces (about 4 handfuls) lettuce, your choice (we prefer butter lettuce)

2 tomatoes, sliced

Slice the tofu into ¼-inch-thick rectangles. Neatly set the rectangles on a clean cloth napkin or dishtowel and fold it over. Wrap the folded dishtowel with another dishtowel and set aside for 30 to 60 minutes. This process pulls some of the water out of the tofu slices, making them thirsty for the marinade.

Place the marinade in a large bowl. Unwrap the tofu slices, place in the marinade, and soak for at least 1 hour—the longer the better.

Preheat the oven to 350°F. Line a baking sheet with parchment paper.

Take the tofu slices out of the marinade and place onto the lined pan. Bake for 30 to 45 minutes, until browned and a bit chewy. Your call, the longer they cook the chewier the tofu gets.

At the end of the tofu baking time, toast your bread, if that is your preference. Construct each BLT&A by spreading some mashed avocado on two slices of bread, then add a layer of tofu, a heap of lettuce, a layer of sliced tomatoes, a few slices of avocado, and finally, a top layer of bread. Wrap two hands around this one and don't let go until it is done.

V-EGG SALAD SANDWICH

When our mom tasted this she winced and said, "Uh-oh, what is this? It tastes like egg salad." Her suspicion was correct! But it's a **V**eggie version of **E**gg salad: V-Egg Salad! We like to heap it on crispy rye toast with a spoonful of mango salsa on top! Or why not use crackers or romaine to scoop the salad up as a dip?

Makes about 3 cups

12 ounces silken firm tofu, cut into ¼-inch cubes

⅓ red onion, chopped

1 cup chopped celery

½ cup Homemade Hummus (page 67) or store-bought hummus with no added oil or tahini

2 tablespoons dried dill, or chopped fresh dill

1 dill pickle, chopped, or more to taste

2 tablespoons Dijon mustard

1 tablespoon lemon juice

¼ teaspoon turmeric

Black pepper, to taste

4 slices 100% whole rye bread or 100% whole-grain bread, toasted

Brando Mango Salsa (page 86)

Place the tofu cubes on a clean kitchen towel to drain, for 10 to 20 minutes.

In a bowl, combine the onion, celery, hummus, dill, chopped pickle, mustard, lemon juice, turmeric, and black pepper to taste, and mix.

Unwrap the tofu cubes, add to the bowl, and toss everything together until well mixed.

On top of each piece of toasted rye bread, spread a thick layer of the V-Egg salad and add a dollop of mango salsa right in the center. Delicious!

BELIEVELAND CRISPY WRAP

Our parents, Ann and Essy, have been counseling people on how to prevent and reverse heart disease for over thirty years. When they first started, they invited patients to their house and after several hours of counseling took a lunch break and served a crispy wrap. Now they counsel at the Cleveland Clinic Wellness Institute and that same lunch is served. This is our version of the wrap that has helped convince so many patients that plant-based eating can be delicious. They are best baked until crispy, crispy, crispy.

TIP: Try the wraps with a different hummus or spread and any of your favorite veggies.

Makes 4 wraps

4 whole-grain or rice wraps (aka tortillas), no added oil

1 cup Homemade Hummus (page 67) or store-bought hummus with no added oil or tahini

4 green onions, finely diced

½ cup shredded carrots

1 tomato, chopped

½ cup corn, frozen is fine

¼ cup cilantro, coarsely chopped

¼ cup fresh basil, coarsely chopped (if available)

½ cup strips fresh mango

2 to 3 cups fresh spinach

1 cup broccoli sprouts (optional—but so good for you)

Preheat the oven to 400°F. Line a baking sheet with parchment paper.

Spread each wrap with a layer of hummus. In the center of each wrap, add green onions, carrots, tomato, corn, cilantro, basil, mango, spinach, and sprouts if using. Fold sides over to make a stuffed cigar shape and place on the baking sheet. Secure with toothpicks or a metal skewer if necessary.

Bake for 12 minutes, until crispy, browned, and warm.

Grilled Sandwiches at Home and Pitas to Go

When you want to upgrade your sandwiches, we suggest you spring for a panini sandwich grill. It's a game changer! Each sandwich transforms under the warm influence of the double-sided grill. This single step changes the ordinary into the extraordinary—and makes for a crispy, luscious, sophisticated sandwich!

However, if you are on the go, we suggest you pack what you can into a pita. We learned this from our mom who used to stuff anything—really anything—we had for dinner the night before into a large pita pocket for our father to eat in between surgeries. He would have a pita pocket of mashed potatoes and beets, a pita pocket of lasagna, or a pita pocket of veggie stir-fry! She was fearless about her pita pocket packing and he loved it.

GRILLED ROMESCO ON RYE

After creating a plant-strong Romesco sauce, we had to put it on everything! It changed a regular old rye sandwich into a picnic in the Italian countryside. Grill the sandwich up or have it in a pita to go.

Serves 4

½ cup Romesco Sauce (page 54)

8 slices 100% whole rye bread, or 4 whole wheat pita pockets

1 large tomato, sliced

4 green onions, chopped

1 head romaine lettuce or butter lettuce

1 avocado, sliced (optional)

For grilled sandwiches: Heat up your sandwich grill to medium-high.

Spread 1 tablespoon Romesco onto each piece of bread. To 4 slices, add layers of tomato, green onions, romaine, and avocado if using. Top off each with another piece of Romesco-coated bread.

Place 2 sandwiches into the preheated sandwich grill. Press the lid down gently—you want to heat up the top layer of bread, yet you don't want to squish the sandwich contents right out of the sandwich. Check your sandwiches after 2 to 3 minutes to see if they are grilled to your liking; if not, leave them in for a minute or two longer. Repeat to grill the 2 remaining sandwiches. Slice all the sandwiches in halves, or in quarters to share with friends.

For pitas to go: Spread 1 tablespoon Romesco onto the top and bottom of the pocket of 1 pita. Add layers of tomatoes, green onions, romaine, and avocado if using. Repeat three times, building all 4 pockets.

ANN'S GRILLED GRAND SLAMWICH

We adore our mother and her zest for life and food. She gets so excited and wide-eyed about things that you can't help but get sucked into her vortex of enthusiasm. If there's a sandwich that Ann adores and will never tire of, it's this grilled grand slam. If you are in a hurry, pack it up in a pita to go.

Makes 4 sandwiches

1 cup Homemade Hummus (page 67) or store-bought hummus with no added oil or tahini

8 slices any variety Ezekiel 4:9 bread, or 4 whole wheat pita pockets

4 green onions, chopped

1 large heirloom tomato, cut into 4 thick slices

2 tablespoons Dijon mustard

1 head Boston lettuce

½ to 1 cup Roasted Red Bell Peppers (page 130) or store-bought roasted peppers

For grilled sandwiches: Heat up your sandwich grill to medium-high.

Spread 1 tablespoon hummus onto each piece of bread. To 4 slices, add layers of green onions, tomato, mustard, lettuce, and roasted peppers. Top off each sandwich with another piece of hummus-coated bread.

Place 2 sandwiches on the preheated sandwich grill. Press the lid down gently—you want to heat up the top layer of bread, yet you don't want to squish the sandwich contents right out of the sandwich. Check your sandwiches after 2 to 3 minutes to see if they are grilled to your liking. If not, leave them in for a minute or two longer. Repeat to grill the 2 remaining sandwiches. Slice in halves, or in quarters to share with friends.

For pitas to go: Spread 1 tablespoon of hummus onto the top and bottom of the pocket of 1 pita. Add layers of green onions, tomato, mustard, lettuce, and roasted peppers. Repeat three times, building all 4 pockets.

I am a female African American and due to the history of diabetes in my family, I was heading down that path. At an early age, I began losing my sight for intervals of time. After a visit with my doctor, I was told that these symptoms were a part of the process of early-onset diabetes. No advice was given as to how to reverse what was happening— just a brief look at what was my destiny since it "runs in my family." Family members embraced it, and repeatedly said, "That's just what we do!"

Soon after, I discovered my father had been diagnosed as a "borderline diabetic" and that news hit too close to home! I decided this would not be a generational curse and would not be the norm for my family and me. I had gained weight after my third pregnancy; therefore, I decided to take matters into my own hands. This was when I decided a plant-strong diet would become the choice for our family. Like many others, my research was intense. I watched documentaries and read every piece of material within the arena that would enhance my knowledge. I decided to rewrite the family history for my children, so they wouldn't have to look far to know that it is OK to be different. I want them to understand: The eating style that was considered normal for our family for years does not necessarily deem it the right way. I'm honored to report that I not only lost the excess weight, but I have not lost the sight in my eyes for four years and counting. My children are also extremely healthy and I look forward to enjoying my golden years with them and not forcing them to spend my aging years guiding me around. This decision to become a plant-strong family has impacted our lives in so many ways and we are grateful that we were able to make this a part of our lives.

—CYNTHIA GILDER, MOTHER OF FIVE CHILDREN

SWEE'PEA GRILLED SANDWICH

For those of you who loved Popeye the Sailor Man as much as we did back in the day, you'll remember Swee'Pea as the baby left on Popeye's doorstep. Popeye raises him as his own and calls him *boy-kid.* This sandwich reminds me of the show with its Swee'Pea—sweet potatoes—Popeye's spinach, and the high adventure of the Thai Peanut Butter. Grill this one up or pop the filling into a pita and you are ready to sail the high seas!

TIP: Cook the sweet potato in whatever way works best for you until soft throughout: Bake in a 400°F oven for 45 minutes, or cook in the microwave for 8 minutes. Peel the sweet potato.

Makes 2 sandwiches

¼ cup Thai Peanut Butter (page 64)

4 slices 100% whole-grain bread or rye bread, or 2 whole wheat pita pockets

4 ounces fresh spinach

1 large sweet potato, cooked and sliced into medallions

6 to 8 leaves fresh basil

1 tomato, sliced

For grilled sandwiches: Heat up your sandwich grill to medium-high.

Spread a layer of Thai peanut butter on all 4 slices of bread. On 2 slices, place layers of spinach, sweet potato, basil, and tomato slices, and lay the other slices of bread on top. Place both sandwiches in the preheated sandwich grill. Press the lid down gently—you want to heat up the top layer of bread, but you don't want to squish the sandwich contents right out of the sandwich. Check your sandwiches after 2 to 3 minutes to see if they are grilled to your liking. If not, leave them in for a minute or two longer. Slice in half and set sail!

For pitas to go: Spread a layer of Thai peanut butter on the tops and bottoms of the pockets of the pitas. Inside both pockets, place layers of spinach, sweet potato, basil, and tomato slices.

BUILD-YOUR-OWN GRILLED SANDWICH OR PITA TO GO

Be as fearless as our mom when making these pockets.

TRY USING ANY OF THESE SPREADS:

OMG Walnut Sauce (page 57)

Jalapeño Walnut Sauce and Spread (page 57)

Kale Butter 3.0 (page 58)

Beet Butter (page 61)

Sriracha Carrot Hummus (page 62)

Secretariat Sweet Chile Spread (page 63)

Thai Peanut Butter (page 64)

Ginger-Wasabi Edamame Hummus (page 66)

Garlic Lover's Hummus (page 68)

Thai Curry Hummus and Dip (page 69)

Hatch Green Chile Hummus (page 69)

PILED HIGH WITH YOUR CHOICE OF:

Greens: cilantro, basil, parsley, spinach, kale, Swiss chard, collards, any of your favorites

Cooked asparagus

Corn

Lettuce

Tomato slices

Bell pepper strips

Broccoli sprouts

Cucumber slices

Radish slices

Beet slices

Chopped green onions

Cooked sweet potato rounds

Build your sandwich as fast as a firefighter jumps into bunker-gear! Spread on your hummus or spread of choice, add as many veggies and greens as possible on top, top with second slice of bread and you're good to grill!

BYO PITZAS
(BUILD-YOUR-OWN PITA PIZZAS)

On a clean long surface (counter or table) set up an area for a pizza fixin' bar with:

Toasted whole wheat pitas

Red sauce (no oil added)

Homemade Hummus (page 67)

Romesco Sauce (page 54)

Chopped bell peppers

Roasted Red Bell Peppers (page 130)

Cooked sweet potato rounds

Cooked asparagus

Chopped onions

Chopped broccoli

Cubed pineapple

Sliced mushrooms

Sliced tomatoes

Banana peppers

Nutritional yeast

Chopped basil

Olives

Invite everyone to build their own pitza. Bake the pitzas on a parchment-lined baking sheet in a 350°F oven for about 5 minutes, until all ingredients are warm and the pita is toasty.

Over the last twenty years, I've had more than ten major surgeries from the belly button to pelvis. In addition, I suffered extreme sexual invasion as a child, which affected me greatly. I experienced painful intercourse throughout my relationship with my husband, and menopause diminished my desire tremendously.

I had been told by doctors that I must eat olive oil because of my low weight and to lubricate my body even though I had experienced eight strokes and other vascular issues. Then Jane explained how oil affects the arteries and veins and how eliminating it and eating lots of dark greens repaired it. She also mentioned that plant-based whole foods without salt, sugar, and oil allowed men to have better erections and since that was the same physiology as with women, it may do the same for women. Though I didn't believe for a second it would work for me, given the damage, I listened.

Jay and I started our plant-strong whole foods without SOS diet on the retreat. Our lives were changed. We have also started each day with a big bowl of kale, spinach, Swiss chard, and other dark greens virtually every day since. Even Jay grew to love them.

Three months into the new life, I began feeling sexual desire. It literally shocked me. Four or five months into our new way of eating, we tried intercourse and it didn't hurt—a huge milestone but it also didn't feel good. At nine months, we tried and it felt absolutely wonderful. That was the first time I could remember. I ran around shouting like a kid with a new bicycle! We have made up for lost time and I nearly cry each time because it feels so good. I feel whole. Yes, my salt and oil cravings have disappeared. Yes, I almost never feel famished in the way I did when I ate meat. Yes, our emotional evenness is glorious. But I also have been healed as a woman in ways I can never describe and I am so grateful. Though I originally went to the retreat to support my husband, I was transformed by trying the experiment as it was presented. And believe me, Jay makes sure we never run out of kale!

I want other women to know that being completely sexually healed is possible. Every post-menopausal woman and women who have had multiple female surgeries should know about a whole-food plant-strong food without SOS eating and its potential effect on their sexual healing and pleasure.

—ADELL SHAY, BUSINESS PROFESSOR EMERITUS, AND JAY STINT, PROGRAM DIRECTOR AT MAGO RETREAT, SERVING PLANT-BASED, WHOLE FOOD SINCE MAY 2014

CHAPTER 8

SUPPERS AND ONE-BOWL MEALS

TERRIFIC TERIYAKI TOFU BOWL

This tofu bowl will garner major applause—it's terrific! Beware: You may find yourself eating the tofu cubes like movie popcorn, popping them in your mouth until they all disappear.

TIP: The tofu will turn out best if you allow it to marinate in the teriyaki sauce for a few hours.

Serves 2 or 3

1½ cups brown rice

3 tablespoons sesame seeds

5 tablespoons low-sodium tamari

3 tablespoons 100% pure maple syrup

1 tablespoon tomato paste or ketchup (no high-fructose corn syrup)

2 teaspoons minced fresh ginger

1 14-ounce block firm or extra-firm tofu, cut into ½-inch cubes

1 crown broccoli, broken into florets and steamed

3 green onions, chopped

Prepare rice as directed on package.

In a skillet over medium-low heat, toast the sesame seeds until lightly browned and fragrant, about 5 minutes. Keep a watchful eye as they burn easily. Set aside.

In a large bowl, make the teriyaki sauce: Mix the sesame seeds, tamari, maple syrup, tomato paste, and ginger until well combined. Add the tofu cubes and toss (with hands if the tofu is crumbly) until thoroughly coated. If you have time, let the tofu marinate in the sauce for a few hours.

Preheat the oven to 350°F. Line a baking sheet with parchment paper.

Spread the tofu cubes on the lined pan. Save any extra sauce. Bake for 30 to 40 minutes or until the cubes are browned and luscious looking.

In each of 2 or 3 dinner bowls, place a scoop of brown rice, smother it in tofu cubes, steamed broccoli, and green onions, and drizzle any extra teriyaki sauce on top.

INDIAN-SPICED BASMATI RICE BOWL

Basmati rice, which smells like popcorn when cooking, contributes a special—almost exotic—base to this bowl. Build the bowl high with savory lentils and snappy vegetables to make a taste and texture creation of your own.

Serves 2 to 4

1½ cups brown basmati rice

1 cup dry lentils, or 2 (14-ounce) cans lentils, drained and rinsed

½ cup low-sodium vegetable broth

1 medium carrot, finely chopped

1 cup frozen peas, thawed to room temperature

3 green onions, chopped

¼ teaspoon curry powder (or garam masala), or to taste

⅛ teaspoon cinnamon

⅛ teaspoon ground ginger

2 cups butter lettuce leaves

¼ cup fresh cilantro (or parsley), coarsely chopped (optional)

Prepare the rice as directed on package.

If using dry lentils, place in a medium pot with 4 cups of water. Bring to a boil over high heat, then turn the heat to low and simmer for 20 to 30 minutes, until the lentils are soft through and through. Drain off any extra water. If using canned lentils, place them in a microwaveable bowl and microwave for 60 seconds, then transfer to a medium pot.

Place the pot of lentils over low heat, add the broth, carrot, peas, green onions, curry powder, cinnamon, and ginger and cook, stirring, for 2 to 3 minutes, until heated throughout.

In the base of 2 to 4 large dinner bowls, place a layer of lettuce leaves followed by a layer of rice followed by a layer of lentil curry vegetable mixture. Top it off with a garnish of cilantro. Grab your fork and dive in!

THAI CURRY SWEET-POTATO BOWL

If you have an addiction to Thai food like we do, then you'll flip over this bowl. With its spices, flavors, and a fresh feel, it is delicious. If you've never had Thai food before, this is a perfect plant-strong starter to introduce you to a whole new world of flavor. Be brave—you'll be so glad you tried something new! It is great served with a large green salad.

Serves 4 to 6

2 sweet potatoes

1 large onion, julienned

8 ounces mushrooms, sliced

1 crown broccoli, cut into florets

1 red bell pepper, diced

2 carrots, sliced into thin rounds

1 (8-ounce) can baby corn, drained and rinsed

2 cups plain oat milk

1 tablespoon 100% pure maple syrup

2 to 3 teaspoons green curry paste, your preference (Thai Kitchen makes an oil-free paste)

½ teaspoon coconut extract

6 to 8 leaves fresh basil (or Thai basil if available), finely chopped

Cook the sweet potatoes in whatever way works best for you until soft throughout: Bake in a 400°F oven for 45 minutes, or cook in the microwave for 8 minutes. Peel the sweet potatoes and cut into halves or cubes.

In a large skillet over high heat, cook the onions, slowly reducing the heat and occasionally stirring, until browned, about 5 minutes. Add the mushrooms, broccoli, bell pepper, carrots, and baby corn. Cover and cook the vegetables until their colors turn bright, but they still have snap, about 5 more minutes.

In a saucepan over medium-high heat, combine the milk, maple syrup, curry paste, and coconut extract. Stir until warm and well combined.

Place the halved or cubed sweet potato in the base of 4 to 6 bowls, add the cooked vegetables, and serve with a garnish of basil. If there is any, add a drizzle of extra sauce to the bowls. You will hear a chorus of oohs and ahhs!

DESERTED ISLAND SOBA NOODLE BOWL

This colorful soba bowl is so good that if you were deserted on an island and could only have one dish for the rest of your life, well, this might be the one. It would be for Jane!

Serves 4

12 ounces buckwheat or whole wheat soba noodles

1 cucumber, peeled, seeded, and diced

1 red bell pepper, diced

1 to 2 mangoes, peeled and diced

4 green onions, chopped

½ cup julienned or matchstick carrots

1 avocado, cubed

2 teaspoons minced fresh ginger (or more if you like the flavor-filled heat of ginger)

6 tablespoons low-sodium tamari

5 tablespoons 100% pure maple syrup

3 tablespoons rice vinegar

2 tablespoons sesame seeds

Prepare the soba noodles as directed on package. (We prefer cooking them in a large pot to avoid overflow.) Run the cooked noodles under cold water in a colander so they cool down and won't stick together, then drain.

In a large bowl, combine the noodles, cucumber, bell pepper, mango, green onions, carrots, and avocado and toss.

In a small bowl, combine the ginger, tamari, maple syrup, and vinegar. Stir until uniformly mixed, then pour over the noodles. Toss well.

In a skillet over medium-low heat, toast the sesame seeds, keeping a close eye on them, for about 5 minutes, until they brown slightly and become fragrant.

Sprinkle the toasted sesame seeds over the dressed noodles. Serve immediately (or chill in a covered dish) along with a large green salad!

ECUADORIAN DINNER BOWL

The jalapeño heat and lime notes of the Amazon Dressing perfectly match the vegetables in this fresh, bright, and nutrient-dense bowl. You will love the red quinoa, black beans, corn, tomatoes, peppers, mangoes, avocados, and spinach—basically everything delicious and plant-strong. The bowl includes the taste of Ecuador together with flavor and zing. Instead of the fresh spinach, you could also serve the vegetables over fresh arugula, or alongside a heap of steamed greens.

Serves 4

1 cup red quinoa

1 (15-ounce) can black beans, drained and rinsed

1 cup white sweet corn (frozen is fine)

2 tomatoes, chopped

1 red bell pepper, diced

1 ripe mango, skinned and cubed (or 1 cup frozen mango chunks)

1 avocado, diced or mashed

2 cloves garlic, minced

1 cup Amazon Dressing (page 101)

8 ounces fresh spinach

Cook the quinoa as directed on package. Set aside.

In a large bowl, combine the quinoa, black beans, corn, tomatoes, bell pepper, mango, avocado, and garlic. Stir until well mixed.

Add the dressing and stir. Adjust seasonings to taste: You may want more jalapeño heat or more lime juice kick. Serve immediately over the spinach.

THAI CURRY SWEET-POTATO
BOWL (page 189)

GREEN LIGHTNING BOWL
(page 199)

ECUADORIAN DINNER BOWL
(opposite)

FULFILLING FARRO BOWL

You can think of farro as wheat and barley's older European cousin. Though not everyone has heard of farro, it is super-hearty, power-packed and easy to prepare. Look for it in the bulk section of health food stores, near the quinoa and barley on grocery store shelves, and online.

Serves 2

1 cup farro

1 (15-ounce) can black-eyed peas, drained and rinsed

2 to 4 cups fresh spinach leaves

1 cup thawed frozen shelled edamame

½ red bell pepper, diced

½ cup sliced rinsed canned water chestnuts

1 cup fresh sugar snap peas

1 cup dressing, your favorite (we recommend Dragon Dressing, page 94, or Amazon Dressing, page 101)

In a pot over high heat, combine 3 cups water and the farro and bring to a boil. Turn the heat down to low, cover, and let simmer for 15 minutes, or until all the water is absorbed. Or, if you have a rice cooker that will work just fine. Prepare the farro in the rice cooker or on the stovetop, the ratio is 1 cup farro to 3 cups water.

Place the black-eyed peas in a microwave-safe bowl and microwave for 60 seconds, until warmed throughout. Or, if you prefer the stovetop, place in a small pot and warm over medium-high heat, stirring occasionally, for about 5 minutes, until warmed through and through.

To build your bowls, start with a layer of spinach in the base of each, add a layer of farro, then a layer of black-eyed peas. On top, add edamame, bell pepper, water chestnuts, and sugar snaps and drizzle with dressing.

KICK-ASS SOUTHWESTERN POLENTA BOWL

This bowl covers some serious terrain—from expanses of smooth mellow polenta, to unexpected arroyos of roasted bell peppers, to exciting mesas of black beans and cumin. If you've never had polenta before, you'll totally dig the foundation of this bowl.

Serves 2 to 3

1½ cups corn kernels, frozen is fine

1 medium red onion, finely chopped

2 cloves garlic, finely minced

1 cup Roasted Red Bell Peppers (page 130) or store-bought roasted peppers, finely chopped

1 (15-ounce) can black beans, drained and rinsed

1 teaspoon dried rosemary

¼ teaspoon ground cumin

Pinch or 2 ground cayenne pepper

3 cups water, plus more as needed

1 cup polenta (also known as finely ground cornmeal)

¼ teaspoon dried oregano

Pinch of salt, or to taste (optional)

Ground black pepper, to taste

Hot sauce, to taste (for this bowl, we prefer the Cholula brand)

In a medium skillet, combine the corn, onion, garlic, roasted peppers, beans, rosemary, cumin, and cayenne and cook over medium-high heat for 5 to 10 minutes, until the onions are translucent and the corn is lightly browned. Set aside.

In a soup pot, bring the 3 cups water to a boil. Pour in the polenta and cook, stirring constantly, for 2 to 3 minutes. Reduce the heat to low. Add the oregano, salt if using, and pepper and simmer, stirring every few minutes, for 15 to 20 minutes, until well incorporated. If the consistency of the polenta becomes too thick, add water in ½-cup increments to keep the polenta from sticking. Smash up any lumps you find. (Using a whisk helps prevent lumps from forming.) Remove the pot from the heat. Fold in the corn mixture and serve immediately with your favorite hot sauce.

GREEN LIGHTNING BOWL

Lightning always comes before thunder. Serve this dish to your crew and watch the flash of joy light up their faces followed by a thunder of compliments! Green Lightning delivers on a simple promise—that food can be incredibly simple and incredibly satisfying. Start a storm in your house and cook this one up tonight! The key to the bowl is the Lightning Dressing: It adds the "Ka-boom."

Serves 2 to 4

6 tablespoons low-sodium tamari

¼ cup 100% pure maple syrup

1 14-ounce block firm tofu, cut into bite-size cubes

8 ounces brown rice noodles

2 to 3 tablespoons sesame seeds

6 green onions, diced

4 cups thinly sliced (practically chiffonade) kale

1 avocado, cubed

½ cup cilantro leaves, chopped

1 cup Lightning Dressing (page 91)

Preheat the oven to 400°F. Line a baking sheet with parchment paper.

In a bowl, combine the tamari, maple syrup, and tofu cubes and toss until all the cubes are well coated. Pour onto the lined sheet and bake for 45 minutes, until lightly browned.

Prepare the rice noodles as directed on the package. Set aside.

In a skillet over medium heat, toast the sesame seeds. Keep an eye on them as they toast—I burn every other batch!—until lightly browned and fragrant, about 5 minutes. Remove from heat.

In a mixing bowl, combine the cooked rice noodles, tofu cubes, green onions, kale, avocado, cilantro, and dressing, and toss. Sprinkle the toasted sesame seeds over it and serve immediately, or chill until ready to serve. I promise you will want to make this again and again.

GRILLED WARRIOR POCKETS

This hearty pocket sandwich will rise up and fight your hunger with flavor and nutrient density. It is a warm smile waiting for you to dig in, and such a beautiful crispy pocket you will want to Snapchat a photo right away! A panini grill or similar sandwich grill works best for the pockets, but if you don't have one, you can use a skillet, following the directions for the 12 variations that follow.

We suggest dipping the pockets into your favorite dressing. We love this one with Sandy's Caesar Dressing (page 92).

Makes 2 to 4 tortilla pockets

½ cup **OMG Walnut Sauce (page 57)**

½ cup **cooked brown rice**

½ cup **chopped green onions**

½ cup **Roasted Red Bell Peppers (page 130) or store-bought roasted peppers**

½ cup **white corn, fresh or frozen**

½ cup **canned black beans, drained, rinsed, and fork-smashed**

2 cups **fresh spinach**

2 to 4 **whole-grain or rice tortillas (aka wraps), with no added oil**

Preheat a sandwich grill to medium-high, or heat a skillet over medium heat.

In a bowl, combine the walnut sauce, rice, green onions, roasted peppers, corn, beans, and spinach and mix well.

If using a sandwich grill, place a tortilla in the grill. On half of the tortilla, place half or one-fourth of the filling. Fold the uncovered half of the tortilla over, forming a pocket shaped like a half moon. Press the grill closed gently, allowing the filling to spread evenly throughout the tortilla. After 3 to 5 minutes, check: When the tortilla is brown, crispy, and warm all the way through, it is ready. Repeat with the remaining filling and tortillas.

If using a skillet, add a tortilla to the hot pan. Spread half or one-quarter of the filling on half of the warming tortilla. (Or you can just stack the separate ingredients on the tortilla—that works well, too.) When the tortilla is flexible enough to fold, bend the bare half over the ingredient-loaded other half. Continue cooking until the underside is crispy, then flip and cook the other side until browned and crispy. Repeat with the remaining filling and tortillas.

12 TASTY GRILLED WARRIOR POCKETS

All of these pocket sandwiches follow similar instructions to the Warrior (page 200), using either a sandwich grill or skillet:

1. **ROMEO GRILLED WARRIOR POCKETS:** Romesco Sauce (page 54) with romaine, asparagus, and tomato, with more Romesco for dipping

2. **THREE SISTERS GRILLED WARRIOR POCKETS:** Sriracha Carrot Hummus (page 62) with cooked butternut squash cubes (use frozen, or peel, cube, and bake squash on a parchment-lined pan in a 400°F oven for 30 minutes or until soft), corn, black beans, and cooked quinoa; dipped in Brando Mango Salsa (page 86)

3. **HOT-LANTA GRILLED WARRIOR POCKETS:** Secretariat Sweet Chile Spread (page 63) with black-eyed peas, tomatoes, and green onions; served with hot sauce

4. **TAOS GRILLED WARRIOR POCKETS:** Hatch Green Chile Hummus (page 69) with quinoa, shredded carrots, golden raisins, and fresh spinach; dipped in Sweet Fire Dressing (page 101)

5. **FORTUNE TELLER GRILLED WARRIOR POCKETS:** Ginger-Wasabi Edamame Hummus (page 66) with purple cabbage, red pepper, avocado, and cucumber; dipped in Lightning Dressing (page 91)

6. **HERBY MUSHROOM GRILLED WARRIOR POCKETS:** Homemade Hummus (page 67) with mushrooms, oregano, thyme, parsley, and spinach; dipped in True Grit Gravy (page 79)

7. **PURPLE HAZE WARRIOR POCKETS:** Beet Butter (page 61) with shelled edamame, cucumbers, and chopped kale; topped with Mighty Mango Salsa (page 86)

8. **PORTABELLA GRILLED WARRIOR POCKETS:** Clean and Classic Red Marinara (page 77) with portabella mushrooms, oregano, nutritional yeast, and fresh spinach, with more marinara for dipping

9. **GREEN GRILLED WARRIOR POCKETS:** Kale Butter 3.0 (page 58) with sprouts, chopped kale, cherry tomatoes, and cucumbers; dipped in fresh dressing or topped with Brando Mango Salsa (page 86)

10. **GALLIPOLI GRILLED WARRIOR POCKETS:** Garlic Lover's Hummus (page 68) with sauerkraut and chopped kale; served with Cranberry Salsa (page 89)

11. **NO PROBLEMO GRILLED WARRIOR POCKETS:** Fat-free vegetarian refried beans, black beans, tomato, and romaine; topped with East Side Salsa (page 83) and SoCo Guacamole (page 71)

12. **THAI FLYIN' GRILLED WARRIOR POCKETS:** Thai Peanut Butter (page 64) with broccoli florets, baby corn, and spinach; dipped in Asian Fusion Sauce (page 73)

ROMESCO PIZZA

Some gatherings require unique pizzas for different tastes. That gathering can be a family dinner or a block party! We love the fresh greens and hot pizza taste combination. This pizza will have you receiving compliments and phone calls for the recipe!

Makes one 12-inch pizza or 4 individual pizzas. Serves 4 to 6.

Chicago-Style Pizza Dough (page 207), Engine 2 Plant-Strong Stone Baked 100% Whole Wheat Pizza Crust (found in Whole Foods), or Sami's Bakery Millet and Flax Pizza Crust (available at samisbakery.com)

2 cups Romesco Sauce (page 54)

1 red bell pepper, thinly sliced

¼ to ½ red onion, finely diced

1 cup cherry tomatoes, halved or whole, your call

2 cups fresh arugula

Preheat the oven to 400°F. Line a baking sheet with parchment paper. Bake the pizza crust for 8 minutes, or until the dough rises and browns a bit.

Spread a layer of Romesco sauce over the crust and sprinkle on the bell pepper, red onion, and cherry tomatoes. Spread a wee bit more of the Romesco sauce on the vegetables (this helps the vegetables cook).

Bake the pizza for 8 to 10 minutes, until the crust is browned. Cut or tear up the arugula and sprinkle on the pizza right before slicing and serving.

PESTO PERFECTO PIZZA
(page 206)

PICASSO PIZZA
(opposite)

PICASSO PIZZA

This colorful pie is a masterpiece! Beets and pineapple and broccoli and more come together in an artful array of taste and texture. You'll marvel at what you've created and wish you could hang it over the fireplace for all to admire! Inspiration for this pizza comes from the ever-creative website, TheKitchn.com.

Makes one 12-inch pizza or 4 individual pizzas. Serves 4 to 6.

Chicago-Style Pizza Dough (page 207), Engine 2 Plant-Strong Stone Baked 100% Whole Wheat Pizza Crust (found in Whole Foods), or Sami's Bakery Millet and Flax Pizza Crust (available at samisbakery.com)

4 to 8 ounces oil-free marinara or Clean and Classic Red Marinara (page 77)

½ medium red onion, chopped into half-moon shapes

1 cup sliced cooked beets

1 pint (2 cups) cherry tomatoes, halved, or 1 cup sundried tomatoes if you prefer

1 orange bell pepper, chopped

1 to 2 cups diced pineapple (depending on how much you eat while prepping the pizza)

2 cups broccoli florets, cut into small pieces

Preheat the oven to 400°F. Line a baking sheet with parchment paper. Bake the pizza crust for 8 minutes, or until the dough rises and browns a bit.

Spread the marinara sauce over the pizza crust, leaving an approximate 1-inch border around the edges. Arrange your choice of vegetables in a colorful pattern: classic circular, diagonal, stripes, checkerboard—anything goes.

Return the pizza to the oven and bake until the edges are golden brown, 8 to 10 minutes. Let the pizza cool for a few minutes before slicing and serving.

PESTO PERFECTO PIZZA

Jane made this with a high school anatomy and physiology class that was looking at the effect of diet on heart health. They devoured every bit. Making the heart-healthy pesto topping smells fantastic as the basil blends into the hummus.

Makes one 12-inch pizza or 4 individual pizzas. Serves 4 to 6.

1 cup Homemade Hummus (page 67) or store-bought hummus with no added oil or tahini

2 cups fresh basil leaves

Chicago-Style Pizza Dough (page 207), Engine 2 Plant-Strong Stone Baked 100% Whole Wheat Pizza Crust (found in Whole Foods), or Sami's Bakery Millet and Flax Pizza Crust (available at samisbakery.com)

2 tomatoes, sliced

Preheat the oven to 400°F. Line a baking sheet with parchment paper.

In a food processor or high-speed blender, mix the hummus and basil.

Bake the pizza crust for 8 minutes, until the dough rises and browns a bit. Remove the crust from the oven, spread the pesto over the whole pizza, and top with the tomato slices. Place the pizza back in the oven for 8 to 10 minutes, until it is browned on the edges and the pesto is warmed throughout. Slice and serve.

CHICAGO-STYLE PIZZA DOUGH

Who doesn't love a thick, substantial, Chicago-style pizza every now and then? Most of us do. *Mangia, mangia!*

We prefer to use a whole wheat flour called *white whole wheat*. It is 100 percent whole wheat, but is made from a white wheat berry. We prefer King Arthur Flour's organic white whole wheat flour for baking.

Makes enough dough for 1 (12-inch) pizza or 4 large thick personal pizzas. Serves 4 to 6.

2 cups warm water

1 (¾-ounce) packet active yeast

¼ to ½ teaspoon salt

2 teaspoons 100% fruit apricot jam

4 cups white whole wheat flour, plus about 1 cup for dusting

In a large bowl, combine the water, yeast, salt, and jam and stir gently until the jam dissolves. Wait about 10 minutes until the liquid gets cloudy—which means the yeast is activating. Slowly stir in the flour. Stir until the mixture becomes a single connected mass of dough—pieces do not break off easily but stay connected when you tug at them.

Knead the dough in the bowl for a minute or so, then cover with a moist towel and set aside. Allow the dough to rise for 30 minutes to 2 hours.

Preheat the oven to 400°F and line one or two baking sheets with parchment paper.

Once the dough has risen, punch it down and press out into one big crust. It may be more like 1½ large crusts—do what you would like with the extra: 1) bake, then slice into breadsticks, 2) bake a crust, seal it, and store in the fridge for up to five days, 3) make extra pizza for the next day, or 4) freeze the extra dough.

Or, divide the dough into 4 portions for individual pizzas: On a lightly floured surface, roll the dough out into your favorite shapes: traditional rectangle, personal-size pies, family-style rounds, or wacky shapes.

To prebake the crust, carefully transfer the dough onto the lined sheets. Bake for 8 minutes, or until the dough rises and browns a bit. It will be a deep-dish, thicker style crust unless you really roll it out thin. Remove from the oven and do with it what you will. If you are making pizza, check out our Romesco Pizza, page 203, Pesto Perfecto Pizza, page 206, and Picasso Pizza, page 205).

SCOUT'S HONOR STIR-FRY

The secret to a quick and easy stir-fry is to be like a Boy Scout or Girl Scout and always be prepared. Think ahead with your batch cooking and have your rice and tofu prepped and waiting in the fridge. Have your vegetables chopped and waiting so that pulling together a great meal is a snap. There should be a stir-fry badge: Super-quick stir-fries are a staple in the plant-strong lifestyle and mastery of this skill sets you up for success!

Serves 2 to 4

1 cup long-grain brown basmati rice

12 ounces firm tofu, cubed, any excess water drained

2 to 3 tablespoons low-sodium tamari

1 crown broccoli, cut into florets and then halved

1 cup julienned carrots

3 green onions, chopped

1 red bell pepper, julienned

1 zucchini, sliced into rounds and quartered

Teriyaki Sauce (page 93); double the recipe (you will thank yourself for doing so!)

Prepare the rice as directed on package.

Preheat the oven to 350°F. Line a baking sheet with parchment paper.

Place the tofu cubes on the lined pan. Drizzle tamari on the cubes so they are all a bit colored by the tamari. Bake for 45 minutes, until browned. Set aside to cool.

Meanwhile, cook the broccoli in a pot of boiling water for 1 minute. Drain and immediately rinse under cold water. (This makes the broccoli crisp yet cooked perfectly for a stir-fry.) Set aside.

Heat a wok over high heat until hot enough that water dropped in the wok dances around like a bead. Add the carrots, green onions, and bell pepper all together and stir-fry for a minute. Have a glass of water or a squirt bottle of water at the ready to squirt a bit of water on the mixture if it gets too dry. Add the zucchini and stir-fry for another 2 to 4 minutes—until the zucchini browns a bit as it cooks. Add the tofu and broccoli and stir-fry until all ingredients are warmed throughout. Pour about 1 cup teriyaki sauce into the hot wok and stir until everything is coated.

Serve over the brown rice with extra teriyaki sauce nearby.

My father died from prostate cancer when he was 63. My grandfathers both suffered heart attacks. My mother has dementia. I had a cancerous tumor removed from my bladder at age 41. So many of the disease processes I see appear to be connected to our eating habits, and I could not help but think of the connections this had to my family. I knew some years ago something needed to change for myself, when one of the pilots I work with as a flight medic (a dear friend) announced that my flight suit looked like a leotard on me. I also had to lose at least thirty pounds to keep my job when a new company policy came along in January 2010.

In April 2010, I started making what I felt were dramatic choices about my eating habits. First to go was white bread and all red meat. I gave up eggs and dairy in June. I tried to emphasize whole foods in my meals. I searched for high fructose corn syrup on labels; if it showed up I did not eat it.

I have had nothing but support at the fire department and air medical transport company—I'm not home very much. Having lost over twenty pounds so far, the changes have been positively noticed. I have gone from a tight 44-waist trouser to a comfortable 40. I discovered it is considerably less expensive to eat healthy, simple foods. The traditional diet of fast food for EMS personnel is not only unhealthy it is very expensive.

As I was investigating books on diets back in June, I discovered the Engine 2 Diet. It surprised me that I was almost "Hegan." The book gave me a solid workout that I can work with when on duty that requires no gym equipment as this had been a huge issue for me. The Engine 2 Diet pushed me to drop all meat, almost, as I may have fish when I eat out on rare occasion. I learned how to structure meals quite a bit better and add a greater variety of foods. The simple recipes rock. The book was tremendously encouraging, and I have recommended it highly to coworkers who have since also purchased it.

Got my cholesterol test back only yesterday. Kinda sad that I don't know the baseline of where I started.

Total cholesterol=134

HDL=30

Triglycerides=100

LDL=84

My doctor asked me three times if I was taking medication to lower my cholesterol.

—PAUL GUTEKUNST, FIREFIGHTER

EPIC BRATS

These bratwursts are the creation of Renee Deman, a super enthusiastic and spirited Whole Foods Market store team leader at the Spring Lake Wall store on the New Jersey shore. Renee, who attended an Engine 2 seven-day immersion program in 2012, told me it took her two years to perfect this creation. I was skeptical. A plant-strong brat that doesn't have oil, plant protein isolates, and a ton of salt that is any good? All I have to say is these are insane. Insane! The brown rice spring roll wraps meld into the filling and create a brat that will blow you and your friends away.

Makes 6 to 8 brats

BASE INGREDIENTS

1 (15-ounce) can garbanzo beans (no salt added), drained and rinsed

1 (15-ounce) can pinto beans (no salt added), drained and rinsed

½ cup cooked brown rice

1 cup rolled oats

6 brown rice spring roll wraps (we prefer Happy Pho brand)

Fixings of choice: ketchup, mustard, sauerkraut, lettuce, tomatoes, kale

STYLE INGREDIENTS

Use these for your style of brat: American, Mexican, Italian, Thai, or Indian

American Style

3 tablespoons diced tomato

3 tablespoons diced green or red bell pepper

3 tablespoons diced red onion

2 tablespoons mustard

2 tablespoons diced dill pickles or low-sodium relish

Mexican Style

1 (15-ounce) can black beans (no salt added), drained and rinsed, instead of pinto beans

2 tablespoons salsa

2 tablespoons diced green chilies

2 tablespoons chopped cilantro

2 tablespoons diced bell pepper

1 cup shredded zucchini or squash

Italian Style

1 (15-ounce) can kidney beans (no salt added), drained and rinsed, instead of pinto beans

2 tablespoons diced sundried tomatoes rehydrated in water

2 tablespoons capers or diced olive

1 cup shredded kale

1 tablespoon Italian herbs or just oregano (try ¼ teaspoon fennel seeds if you wish).

Thai Style

1 (15-ounce) can garbanzo beans (no salt added), drained and rinsed, instead of pinto beans

2 tablespoons fresh lime juice

2 tablespoons chopped green onions

2 tablespoons minced fresh ginger root

2 tablespoons minced fresh basil

½ cup shredded savoy cabbage

Sriracha, to taste

Indian Style

2 cups cooked red lentils, instead of pinto beans

2 tablespoons pureed fresh or frozen mango

3 tablespoons small diced red onion

½ cup shredded carrots

½ cup shredded butternut squash

Fresh lime juice, to taste

Place the first 4 base ingredients in a large bowl. Use an immersion blender or a food processor to partially process the ingredients until some beans are halfway smashed and others fully mashed. If you are looking for a good arm workout, mash all the ingredients using a fork.

To the bowl add in the ingredients for American-, Mexican-, Italian-, Thai-, or Indian-style brats, and stir into the mix until well combined.

Place the bowl in the fridge for at least 15 minutes; the longer the better.

In the meantime, set up a rice wrap station with a skillet or deep plate filled with warm water. Remove mixture from the fridge. Place a brown rice spring roll wrap into the warm water and place ⅓ cup mixture in the center of the wrap. With your hands, press the mixture into the shape of a bratwurst: Fold the bottom of the wrap (the side closest to you) up, fold in the sides, and roll it up tight toward the top. Repeat until filling is all used. Chill for another 10 to 15 minutes in the fridge.

Place the brats in a skillet over medium-high heat for 5 to 7 minutes, rotating them every minute and a half. If cooking on a barbeque grill, rotate them every minute or two until the brown rice paper starts to bubble and grill marks appear.

Place the Epic Brats in whole-grain buns and load up with all the fixings.

Over four years ago, my running friend, who is now a four-time Ironman, revealed to me that the reason she had the extra energy to power up the challenging hill we run regularly was that she had been eating a plant-based diet for several weeks. Inspired by her speed and revelations, I returned home from that run and promptly dusted off *The Engine 2 Diet* book I had purchased two years earlier. I read Rip's book and decided I'd give the 28-day challenge a try. Those first few days were a "challenge," but knowing there was a finish line ahead made it easier to commit to the diet. I soon found I was having fun trying Rip's recipes: the colors, the textures, and the flavors were so exciting and stimulating to my palate.

Over the course of the next few weeks, I felt a transformation take place in my body—I started feeling cleaner both inside and out! To best describe how I felt to my friends, I compared the inside of my body to the glistening interior of a freshly cut red pepper! I no longer felt the heaviness of food sitting in my stomach. I seemed healthier, lighter, and energized.

It's going on five years and I continue to be plant-strong. With no desire to cross the 28-day finish line, this has become a way of life!

—SUSAN KAYEUM, WEST HARTFORD, CONNECTICUT

UP AND AT 'EM BURGERS

These are the cure for what ails you! Packed with the healing powers of vitamin C–filled sweet potatoes, anti-inflammatory oats and turmeric, antibacterial garlic, blood-vessel-healthy balsamic vinegar, and a flavorful blend of chili powder and smoked paprika, these plant-strong burgers will get you up and at 'em!

Makes 6 to 8 burgers

1 cup cooked sweet potato

1 cup cooked brown rice

1 cup old-fashioned oats

1 (15-ounce) can chickpeas, drained and rinsed (or 1½ cups chickpeas made from dried chickpeas)

4 ounces fresh spinach

2 large cloves garlic, finely minced

1 tablespoon balsamic vinegar

1 tablespoon of your favorite barbecue sauce (we prefer Bone Suckin' Sauce)

1 teaspoon chili powder

¼ teaspoon turmeric

¼ teaspoon smoked paprika

6 to 8 whole-grain buns

Fixings of choice: sliced tomatoes, sliced onions, lettuce, ketchup, mustard, pickles, grilled pineapple, sauerkraut

Cook the sweet potatoes in whatever way works best for you until soft throughout: Bake in a 400°F oven for 45 minutes, or cook in the microwave for 8 minutes. Peel the sweet potatoes and cut into halves or cubes.

In a large bowl, smash together the sweet potato, rice, oats, chickpeas, spinach, garlic, balsamic vinegar, barbecue sauce, chili powder, turmeric, and paprika using a spoon, potato masher, or your hands. (We recommend using your hands as it is fun to watch the big spinach leaves break and shred into beautiful green pieces throughout the burger mix.) Smash as many beans as you can until the mixture sticks together well and you can form burgers.

Form the mixture in 6 to 8 patties that are 3 inches in diameter and ½ inch to ¾ inch thick.

Heat a skillet over medium-high heat. Add the patties and cook until browned on the bottom, about 5 minutes. Flip and brown the other side—about 5 minutes. Serve on whole-grain buns with your favorite burger fixings.

"YO, ADRIAN" BURGERS

These burgers know how to pack a punch! They are that good. Their creator, Char Nolan, is a native of Philly who loves to climb the Museum of Art steps and dance around the Rocky statue! When Rip was in Philly, Char dropped him off at the base so he could run up and down the steps and raise his arms next to Rocky—you know the soundtrack was blaring in his mind when, fists raised, he yelled, "Yo, Adrian."

Makes 6 to 8 burgers

2 tablespoons flaxseed meal

¼ cup warm water

1 medium sweet potato, grated (generous 1 cup)

1 cup old-fashioned oats

1 cup oat flour

1 small red onion, minced (about ½ cup)

2 to 3 cloves garlic, finely minced

2 tablespoons hot sauce

2 tablespoons cider vinegar

2 teaspoons low-sodium tamari

2 teaspoons dried oregano

2 teaspoons dried basil

2 cups finely chopped fresh kale

6 to 8 100% whole-grain buns, toasted

Fixings of choice: sliced tomatoes, sliced onions, lettuce, ketchup, mustard, pickles, grilled pineapple, sauerkraut

Preheat the oven to 400°F. Line a baking sheet with parchment paper; and set aside two 18-inch pieces of parchment to help roll out the burger mixture.

In a small bowl, mix the flaxseed meal and water together. Set aside.

In a mixing bowl, combine the sweet potato, oats, and oat flour and mix well with your hands. Add the onion and garlic and mix well. Add the hot sauce, vinegar, tamari, oregano, and basil and mix again. Add the kale and mix well. Pour in the flax mixture and mix all ingredients by hand. Add up to 2 tablespoons water if the mixture needs more moisture. Allow ingredients to "proof" (a fancy term for *wait and let it do its thing*) for 10 to 15 minutes.

Place the mixture on one piece of parchment paper and place the second piece on top. With a rolling pin, roll out to a ¾-inch thickness. With a 3-inch biscuit cutter (or 3-inch-wide mug), cut out 6 to 8 patties.

Place the formed burgers onto the lined baking sheet and bake for 15 to 20 minutes. Remove from the oven and flip the burgers. Using a spatula, flatten them until they are ½ inch thick. Return the flipped burgers to the oven and bake for an additional 15 minutes, until golden brown. They'll be golden brown and deliciously crispy. Enjoy on toasted, whole-grain buns, alone or with your favorite condiments and plant-strong fixings and a side salad.

TWO-HANDED SLOPPY JOES

A proper sloppy joe requires two hands, a big appetite, and focus. If you dare to put your sloppy joe down it is hard to pick up again! So load up with napkins and lean over your plate while you devour this American favorite. We stand by these joes. We also like to make a smoky, sloppy twist on shepherd's pie by topping the filling here with the mashed potatoes from our Sensational Shepherd's Pie (page 232).

NOTE: If you are not using canned lentils, combine 1½ cups dry lentils and 4 cups water in a pot. Bring to a boil then simmer for 20 minutes, until the lentils are soft. Drain if necessary.

Serves 4

1 medium onion, diced

2 cloves garlic, minced

1 green bell pepper, diced

1 cup mushrooms, sliced

1 (6-ounce) can tomato paste

1 (15-ounce) can diced tomatoes, drained

3 cups cooked brown lentils, or 2 (15-ounce) cans lentils, drained and rinsed

¼ cup barbecue sauce (we prefer Bone Suckin' Sauce)

1 tablespoon 100% pure maple syrup

¼ teaspoon liquid smoke, or ¼ teaspoon smoked paprika

2 teaspoons chili powder

4 whole-grain buns

Fixings: butter lettuce, sliced tomato, sliced red onion

In a skillet over medium heat, cook the onion, garlic, bell pepper, and mushrooms until soft and slightly browned, about 5 minutes. Add the tomato paste and diced tomatoes and continue to cook and stir over low heat until all warmed and mixed together, about 3 minutes. Add the cooked lentils, barbecue sauce, maple syrup, liquid smoke, and chili powder, and thoroughly mix. Reduce the heat and simmer for 5 more minutes. Taste and tweak mixture to your liking: Add more maple syrup for a sweeter flavor, or more barbecue sauce for a smokier or more fiery flavor.

Load the filling onto your whole-grain buns and add your preferred fixings.

HEY DAAL

There is something about a good daal that is satisfying to the core. As this dish simmers your whole house will smell rich, adventurous, and scrumptious. Serve with brown rice on a bed of greens. If there is any daal left over, think about having it for breakfast.

Serves 6

1 red onion, diced

4 cloves garlic, minced

1 tablespoon minced fresh ginger

1 teaspoon cumin seeds

1 teaspoon ground turmeric

1 teaspoon curry powder

3 skinny green chiles, also called finger chiles (½ a seeded and diced jalapeño pepper will also work)

1 (15-ounce) can diced tomatoes, or 2 tomatoes, diced

⅓ cup cilantro, chopped coarsely

4 cups low-sodium vegetable broth

1 cup red lentils

1 to 2 tablespoons lime juice, to taste

In a large skillet, cook the onions over high heat, stirring constantly and gradually reducing the heat to medium, until soft and translucent, 3 to 5 minutes. Add the garlic, ginger, cumin seeds, turmeric, and curry powder and stir to allow the spices to bloom a few minutes as they heat up. Add the whole green chiles (yes, whole and intact—not chopped up) or the diced jalapeño, the diced tomatoes, and cilantro and stir for a minute or two.

Add the broth and red lentils and raise the heat to medium-high. Once it comes to a boil, reduce the heat and simmer for 40 to 45 minutes, until the lentils soften and the liquid is almost all absorbed. Remove the green chiles if the daal is hot enough for you; if it's not, stir the chiles around a bit so they can deliver more heat. Stir in the lime juice and serve.

SANDBURG BLUE RIDGE CHILI

After our grandmother died, our grandfather, Barney Crile, married Blue Ridge Mountain resident Helga Sandburg, who was also the daughter of Carl Sandburg, the American poet. Helga's daughter, Paula, makes an amazing chili. The first time we had Paula's chili we ate it so slowly—wanting it to last forever, like a great Carl Sandburg poem. Be sure to cut all the vegetables the same size. A great deal of the liquid comes from the tomatoes so canned tomatoes work best. Serve the chili by itself or with rice and a lovely salad.

Serves 12

2 to 3 large onions, chopped (about 4 cups)

6 medium carrots, cut into ½-inch pieces

6 cloves garlic, chopped (2 tablespoons)

3 tablespoons chili powder

2 tablespoons ground cumin

2 medium sweet potatoes, cut into ½-inch pieces

3 bell peppers, red, green, and yellow, cut into ½-inch pieces

2 (28-ounce) cans whole peeled tomatoes

1 (6-ounce) can tomato paste

2 teaspoons dried oregano

1 teaspoon fennel seeds

2 medium yellow squash, halved and cut into ½-inch pieces

2 medium zucchini, halved and cut into ½-inch pieces

1 (15-ounce) can black beans, drained and rinsed

1 (15-ounce) can kidney beans, drained and rinsed

2 cups fresh parsley, coarsely chopped

½ to 1 teaspoon black pepper

Grated zest of 1 lemon

2 tablespoons lemon juice

2 tablespoons barbecue sauce, or to taste (we prefer Bone Suckin' Sauce)

1 to 2 tablespoons balsamic vinegar

In a large soup pot over medium heat, cook the onions and carrots, stirring, for 7 minutes, until browned and fragrant. Add water or broth as necessary. Add the garlic and cook for about 3 minutes, continuing to stir. Reduce the heat to low and stir in chili powder and cumin and cook another minute. Stir in the sweet potatoes, bell peppers, tomatoes, tomato paste, oregano, and fennel seeds and bring to a boil over medium-high heat. Reduce the heat to medium-low, partially cover, and simmer, stirring occasionally, for 25 minutes.

Add the yellow squash, zucchini, black beans, kidney beans, parsley, and black pepper and simmer, uncovered and stirring occasionally, for 20 minutes longer, until the vegetables are tender. Stir in the lemon zest and juice, barbecue sauce, and balsamic vinegar to taste.

DEBOOM'S IRONMAN CHERRY CHILI

Rip's friend Tim DeBoom won the coveted Hawaii Ironman triathlon twice, in 2001 and 2002. The first time, right after 9/11, he broke a five-year streak of no American winning the race. Rip will never forget the vision of Tim crossing the finish line waving the American flag. Tim and his wife, Nicole, made this chili for Rip one night when he crashed at their place. After two bites he couldn't get over how much he loved cherries in chili. It's a total winner—just like they are!

Serves 8

¼ cup dried tart cherries

2 medium sweet potatoes, peeled and cubed

1 medium onion, chopped

1 red bell pepper, chopped

3 cloves garlic, finely minced

1 cup Roasted Red Bell Peppers (page 130) or store-bought roasted peppers, chopped

2 tablespoons chili powder

2 teaspoons dry mustard

1 teaspoon ground cumin

1 (28-ounce) can diced fire-roasted tomatoes, with juice

3 cups low-sodium vegetable broth

1 (15-ounce) can black beans, drained and rinsed

1 (15-ounce) can kidney beans, drained and rinsed

½ cup sweet corn, frozen is fine

1 cup fresh cilantro, chopped

1 jalapeño pepper, seeded and diced, for topping

Place the cherries in a dish of warm water and let soak for 2 to 3 minutes. Drain and try to rinse off any of the oil used in processing the dried cherries. Repeat, soaking, draining, and rinsing the cherries again. Set aside.

Microwave or steam the sweet potato cubes until they are soft, and set aside.

In a large pot over medium heat, cook the onion and bell pepper in a little water until soft, about 5 minutes. Add the garlic and cook, stirring, for 2 to 3 minutes, until fragrant.

Add the roasted pepper, chili powder, mustard, cumin, tomatoes, and broth. Cook for 2 to 3 minutes over medium heat as the flavors meld together. Increase to high heat and bring the mixture to a boil, then reduce to medium-low heat and simmer for 5 minutes.

Add the drained cherries, steamed sweet potatoes, black beans, kidney beans, corn, and half the cilantro. Continue cooking and stirring on medium-low heat for at least 10 minutes, until well incorporated and the flavors mingle. Simmering longer does not hurt when it comes to chili as long as you remember to stir occasionally.

Serve with remaining cilantro and diced jalapeño to your liking. It is also delicious over brown rice.

1-2-3 VEGETABLE LASAGNA

Did you go overboard at the farmers' market and buy too many vegetables? Have a fridge full of leftovers and a hungry crowd to feed? Throw it all in this lasagna—all but the kitchen sink!

The lasagna is made in basically three steps: 1. Cook veggies. 2. Make tofu filling. 3. Assemble and bake lasagna. These stages can all happen at completely different times or in one cooking session. If I do it at three different times, it does not seem like a great deal of work. Warning: This lasagna is huge. Use proper lifting technique when transferring into and out of the oven.

Serves 12

VEGETABLES

2 large or 3 medium sweet potatoes

1 teaspoon garlic powder

1 tablespoon 100% pure maple syrup

1 large onion, diced (about 1½ to 2 cups)

8 ounces mushrooms, sliced

1 red or orange bell pepper, diced

2 medium zucchinis, sliced (about 3 cups)

2 carrots, chopped

1 (16-ounce) package frozen spinach

1 crown broccoli, cut into florets (about 2 cups)

1 teaspoon dried oregano

1 teaspoon dried basil

1 teaspoon crushed rosemary

TOFU FILLING

1 (15-ounce) package firm tofu, drained

2 tablespoons nutritional yeast

1½ teaspoons onion powder

1½ teaspoons garlic powder

1 teaspoon dried oregano

1 teaspoon dried basil

ASSEMBLY

2 (8-ounce) packages whole wheat lasagna noodles

3 (25-ounce) jars marinara sauce with no added oil, or 7 cups Clean and Classic Red Marinara (page 77)

½ cup cherry tomatoes, halved

Fresh basil for garnish

1. Cook the vegetables: Peel and boil the sweet potatoes for 15 minutes, until soft, or bake the unpeeled potatoes in a 400°F oven for 45 to 60 minutes, until soft, then peel. Place the sweet potatoes in a small bowl, add the garlic powder and maple syrup, and smash with a fork until lump-free and smooth. Set the sweet potato mixture aside. Turn off the oven until ready to cook the whole lasagna.

In a large skillet over high heat, cook the onion until soft and translucent, about 3 minutes, all the while reducing the heat to medium high. Add the mushrooms and continue to cook and stir until they have decreased in size, about 5 minutes. Add the bell pepper, zucchini, carrots, spinach, and broccoli and continue to stir another 5 minutes. Add the oregano, basil, and rosemary and stir a few more times. Remove from the heat and set aside.

2. Make the tofu filling: In a bowl, combine the tofu, nutritional yeast, onion powder, garlic powder, oregano, and basil and fork-smash until crumbly. This creates a ricotta-like texture. Set the tofu aside.

3. Assemble and bake the lasagna: Preheat the oven to 350°F.

In a large bowl, combine the cooked vegetables and tofu filling. Gently mix, using your hands (if the vegetables are cool enough) to prevent the vegetables from getting too crushed and allowing the color of the mixture to stay white in places.

In the bottom of a 14-inch lasagna pan, spread the sweet potato mixture. Place a layer of uncooked noodles on top and pour about one-fourth (about 1½ to 2 cups) of the marinara sauce on top of the noodles. Arrange half of the vegetable-tofu mixture on top of the marinara, then arrange a layer of noodles on top of the veggies. Pour more marinara on top of the noodles and spread the remaining vegetable-tofu mixture on top. Place another layer of noodles on top of the tofu mixture. And finally spread a layer of marinara on top of the noodles and garnish with basil and cherry tomatoes.

Cover the lasagna with a sheet of aluminum foil. Bake for 60 minutes. Remove the foil and cook for 10 more minutes, until the top looks baked not wet. The lasagna is best if cooled for a bit before serving.

LASAGNA MEXICANA

This noodle-free lasagna is easy to make, super-fast, and will satisfy even the pickiest eaters. Make it when you feel like a change of pace from a traditional lasagna with noodles. Change up the layers by adding mushrooms, squash, roasted green chiles (if you live in New Mexico!), or even add olives on top. Serve with SoCo Guacamole (page 71), and Corn Chips (page 132) or Taco Shells or Tostados (page 131).

Serves 8

1 large green bell pepper, chopped

½ jalapeño pepper, seeded and finely chopped (optional)

1 large onion, chopped

2 cloves garlic, minced

2 (15-ounce) cans black beans

2 (15-ounce) cans fat-free vegetarian refried beans

2 medium tomatoes, diced

2 teaspoons chili powder

1 teaspoon ground cumin

3½ cups salsa, your favorite

24 corn tortillas, or more for good measure

2 cups corn, fresh or frozen

Fresh cilantro, for garnish

Hot sauce, your choice

Preheat the oven to 375°F.

In a skillet over high heat, cook the bell peppers, jalapeño, onion, and garlic for about 3 minutes, until softened. Add the black beans, refried beans, tomatoes, chili powder, and cumin.

Pour a generous 1 cup salsa in the bottom of a 9x13-inch baking pan. Cover the salsa with tortillas. Make sure to cover the entire bottom of the pan. It may be necessary to cut some tortillas to fit. Spread half of the bean mixture evenly over the layer of tortillas. On top of the bean mixture add a layer of tortillas. Spread all the corn evenly over the corn tortillas. Add another layer of tortillas on top of the corn.

Continue the pattern from the beginning: Add salsa, tortillas, the remaining bean mixture, tortillas, and the remaining salsa over the tortillas.

Cover the lasagna with foil and bake for about 30 minutes, until hot throughout. Garnish with fresh cilantro. The lasagna will be easier to cut if you allow it to cool for about 10 minutes before serving. Don't forget the hot sauce!

8-MINUTE BLACK BEAN AND RICE DINNER

Tuesday night swim practice and overdue book reports won't stop you from serving up a plant-strong dinner! If you batch cooked your rice and have frozen brown rice on hand (or started your rice cooker before work), you can get dinner to the table in record time. The beans are ready in the can, and only the romaine needs to be chopped: Dinner will be up in less than 8 minutes.

NOTE: To make your rice before work, place 2 cups brown rice and 4 cups water in your rice cooker and press start. When you get home the rice will be cooked. If you use the stovetop and not a rice cooker, it will take 30 to 40 minutes for the rice to cook and dinner to be ready.

Serves 4 to 6

2 (15-ounce) cans black beans, drained and rinsed

1 ¼ cups salsa, your favorite

1 teaspoon barbecue sauce, your favorite

¼ to ½ teaspoon ground cumin

Pinch cayenne pepper

4 cups cooked brown rice

1 to 2 heads romaine lettuce, chopped

Any other vegetables on hand

In a soup pot, combine the beans, ¼ cup of the salsa, the barbecue sauce, cumin, and cayenne. Cook over medium heat until warm through and through.

You are ready to fill bowls and bellies. Place rice on the bottom of each serving bowl, add the beans, top with romaine (and any vegetables), then garnish with the remaining salsa.

AWARD-WINNING BLACK BEANS

If we held a firehouse bean competition, these pulses (*pulse* is a fancy word for beans, lentils, and legumes) would take top prize, no doubt. It took Jane years to want to cook dried beans. Years. It seemed intimidating, time consuming, and confusing. It is none of those! Now she wants to press rewind, go back, and use them over and over again. The texture and flavor cannot be beat. Serve warm with rice, potatoes, quinoa, Taco Shells or Tostados (page 131), or Corn Chips or Rice Chips (page 132) and the fantastic Mighty Mango Salsa (page 86). Or use in tacos, quesadillas, burritos, and salads, as a side, or (with a bit of extra seasoning) as a dip.

NOTE: Cooking dried beans takes 2 to 3 hours, very little of which is active cooking that needs attention.

Serves 8 to 10

1 pound dried black beans

1 onion, diced

8 cloves garlic, minced

2 ancient sweet red peppers (or red bell peppers), seeded and diced

2 bay leaves

½ teaspoon salt (optional)

½ teaspoon ground cumin

¼ teaspoon chili powder

1 tablespoon lime juice

In a large soup pot over high heat, combine 12 cups water, the beans, onion, garlic, peppers, bay leaves, and salt (if using). Bring to a boil, reduce the heat, and simmer for 2½ hours plus or minus 30 minutes (every stovetop simmers a bit differently), until the beans are soft throughout. The majority of the water should be cooked off and the beans coated with a thick broth. Stir in the cumin, chili powder, and lime juice, then turn off heat. Remove and discard the bay leaves.

Using an immersion blender (or food processor or high-speed blender), blend the beans until they are a bit creamy, yet still have texture, like a chunky hummus.

KILLER KABOBS

The next time it's a beautiful sunny day, fire up the grill, invite your not-yet-plant-strong friends over, and make these killer kabobs. You won't regret it and your friends will love you for it. Sometimes we need a delicious nudge to help us change.

Serves 8

---

3 (14-ounce) blocks firm or extra-firm tofu, cut into 1-inch cubes

2 ¼ cups Teriyaki Sauce (page 93), triple the recipe

2 cups brown rice

8 ounces whole white mushrooms

1 sweet onion, cut into 1-inch wedges

1 red onion, cut into 1-inch wedges

2 red bell peppers, cut into 1x1-inch pieces

8 ounces cherry or grape tomatoes

1 (16-ounce) jar barbecue sauce, your favorite (we prefer Bone Suckin' Sauce)

Place the tofu cubes in a large bowl, pour over the teriyaki sauce, and toss. Cover and let the cubes marinate in the sauce for 2 to 3 hours if possible. Toss the cubes once or twice while marinating.

Cook the rice according to package directions within an hour of the meal so it will be warm.

Heat about ½ inch water in a skillet over high heat. Place the whole mushrooms into the water and cook for about 5 minutes. This step makes the mushrooms more flexible and less likely to split when you thread them onto the kabobs.

Fire up your grill. Lay out the tofu, mushrooms, onions, peppers, and tomatoes and begin building the killer kabobs onto 24 or more wooden or metal skewers. We recommend placing larger vegetables like onion sections and peppers on the ends so the tofu in the center is less likely to stick to the grill.

Grill the kabobs for about 15 minutes, anointing them with barbecue sauce once or twice, while rotating frequently—to allow all sides to get blackened.

Serve atop brown rice, with a great green salad.

Tip: At the end of the night, combine all the remaining uncooked vegetables and tofu onto skewers and grill them up. They make amazing leftovers for lunch the next day—even if your skewer has all onions and peppers.

SENSATIONAL SHEPHERD'S PIE

This is an old favorite with a few fun twists. If you are feeling adventurous, try using other fillings, like the one from Two-Handed Sloppy Joes (page 217) or Party On Taco Bar (page 239), as the base of the pie for a delicious change in flavor profile.

Serves 6 to 8

MASHED POTATO TOPPING

10 to 12 medium Yukon Gold potatoes, cut into 1-inch pieces

¾ cup nutritional yeast

5 cloves garlic, minced

4 cups oat milk or almond milk

2 teaspoons dried rosemary

Black pepper to taste

FILLING

1 onion, diced

3 cloves garlic, finely minced

12 ounces mushrooms, sliced

2 cups low-sodium vegetable broth

2 teaspoons white miso

2 tablespoons oat flour (or whole wheat flour)

2 tablespoons low-sodium tamari

2 carrots, chopped (about ½ cup)

2 stalks celery, chopped (about 1 cup)

1 cup peas, frozen are fine

1 cup broccoli florets

½ teaspoon dried thyme

½ teaspoon dried rosemary

½ teaspoon dried sage

Black pepper to taste

Preheat the oven to 350°F.

To make the mashed potatoes: Place the potatoes in a large pot and cover with water. Bring to a boil, reduce the heat, and simmer until tender, about 10 minutes. Drain, place in a large bowl, and mash with a potato masher, eggbeater, or fork. Add the nutritional yeast, garlic, and milk and mash more until smooth. You may need to add a bit more liquid than you expect since the nutritional yeast soaks up some of it. Stir in the rosemary and black pepper to taste.

To make the filling: In a skillet over medium-high heat, cook the onion, stirring frequently, for 5 minutes, until browned. Add a splash of water

to the pan if the onion starts to burn. Add the garlic and mushrooms and continue cooking until the mushrooms soften, about 5 more minutes. Again, add teaspoons of water, as needed, to keep the mixture from burning. Add 1 cup of the broth to the skillet and stir.

To the remaining cup of broth, stir in the miso, flour, and tamari until dissolved. Add the dissolved miso and flour mixture to the pan and simmer, stirring occasionally, for 3 to 5 minutes, until the mixture thickens into gravy. Add the carrots, celery, peas, broccoli, thyme, rosemary, and sage. Season with black pepper to taste.

In a 9×13-inch or 3-quart baking dish or cast iron pan, spread the filling on the bottom, then top with the mashed potatoes. (If your baking dishes or pans are smaller, use more than one for the recipe. This way you will have a pan of leftovers from the start!) Bake for 30 minutes, until the potatoes brown on top. Serve warm.

MAC-N-CASH

Our favorite Macaroni and Not Cheese from *The Engine 2 Diet* book has grown up a bit. And this version is pure money in the bank. Cha-ching!

Serves 4

8 ounces whole-grain elbow pasta

1 onion, chopped

1 cup cashews

¼ cup lemon juice

1½ cups oat milk

½ teaspoon sea salt

½ cup Roasted Red Bell Peppers (page 130), or 1 (4-ounce) jar roasted peppers, drained

¾ cup nutritional yeast

1 teaspoon garlic powder

1 teaspoon onion powder

1 cup roasted corn, frozen or fresh

2 crowns broccoli, chopped into bite-size florets

1 cup collard greens, chopped into inch-long, fine ribbons (optional)

Preheat the oven to 425°F.

Cook the pasta according to directions on package. Drain.

In a skillet over high heat, cook the onion for 3 to 5 minutes, until translucent.

In a food processor, combine the onion, cashews, lemon juice, oat milk, and salt and blend until smooth. Gradually add the roasted peppers, nutritional yeast, garlic powder, and onion powder and blend until the liquid is smooth and red-orange in color.

In a bowl, combine the cooked pasta with the sauce and thoroughly toss them together. Add the roasted corn, broccoli, and collard greens.

Pour the mixture into a family-size baking dish and bake for 20 minutes, or until golden brown on top.

FULL HOUSE POTATO BAR

Here's the deal: If you have great sauces and toppings, it's easy to eat plant-based. This is a full house of sauces and toppings to decorate and then gobble up those moist and rich Yukon Gold potatoes. No one will want to walk away from this packed feast that is bursting with colors and flavors.

Serves 6 to 8 (hopefully with loads of leftovers!)

12 Yukon Gold potatoes

True Grit Gravy (page 79)

Cranberry Salsa (page 89)

Mighty Mango Salsa (page 86)

Jalapeño Walnut Sauce and Spread (page 57)

Romesco Sauce (page 54)

Kale Butter 3.0 (page 58)

Beet Butter (page 61)

8 ounces fresh spinach or romaine lettuce, chopped

2 to 3 tomatoes, diced

4 green onions, finely diced

Salsa, your favorite

Hot sauce, your favorite

Preheat the oven to 400°F.

Two hours ahead of dinner, bake the potatoes in a 400°F oven for 45 minutes to 1 hour. Turn the oven off and leave them in there with the heat off for about an hour; this keeps them warm, yet moist.

Place the potatoes in a handsome bowl or on a platter at the head of the bar and line up the rest of your beautiful sauces and toppings and let everyone create their own wonders!

EXPLODING BURRITO BAR

This explosion of burrito ingredients makes six to eight burritos, depending on the size of your burro (*burro* means "donkey" and *burrito* means "little donkey"). The number of salsas and sauces is up to you—the more the better!

Makes 6 to 8 burritos

8 whole wheat or rice tortillas

1 (15-ounce) can fat-free vegetarian refried beans

1 (15-ounce) can black beans, drained and rinsed

1 (15-ounce) can pinto beans, drained and rinsed

1 sweet potato, cooked, peeled, and cubed

1 red bell pepper, diced

1 tomato, diced

1 head romaine lettuce, chopped

4 green onions, chopped

2 cups cooked brown rice

Roasted Corn Salsa (page 84)

Pico de Gallo (page 87)

Brando Mango Salsa (page 86)

SoCo Guacamole (page 71)

Lovely Sauce (page 72)

Hot sauce of choice

Preheat the oven to 300°F. Wrap the tortillas in foil and place in the oven for 10 minutes, or until ready to use.

In three different small pots over medium-low heat, warm up the refried beans, black beans, and pinto beans. Place the sweet potato, bell pepper, tomato, romaine, and green onions in separate bowls.

Have each guest create an exploding burrito, starting with a warm tortilla and adding rice, beans, and vegetables, along with all the beautiful salsas and sauces you've made. Boom—you won't believe the size of everyone's creations and their exclamations of joy.

PARTY ON TACO BAR

Just like the Full House Potato Bar (page 236), this is a feast for a big family or a group of people with varying tastes. Everyone gets to build their own tacos by piling on their choice of colorful, fun ingredients, toppings, salsas, and sauces. Make it a party.

TIP: Use romaine lettuce leaves as shells and do away with the taco shells.

Serves 6 to 8

1 large sweet onion, diced (3 to 4 cups)

2 cloves garlic, minced

½ jalapeño pepper, seeded and minced

1 red bell pepper, diced

3 cups cooked brown lentils, or 2 (15-ounce) cans lentils, drained and rinsed

¼ cup taco seasoning (we prefer Durkee or Ortega 40% Less Sodium brands)

1 (15-ounce) can fat-free vegetarian refried beans

1 to 2 cups low-sodium vegetable broth

10 to 12 corn tortillas, warmed until soft or made into Taco Shells or Tostados (page 131)

TOPPINGS AND SALSAS

1 head romaine lettuce, chopped

2 tomatoes, chopped

1 medium red onion, chopped

SoCo Guacamole (page 71)

East Side Salsa (page 83)

Pico de Gallo (page 87)

Mighty Mango Salsa (page 86)

Toasted Pepitas (page 152)

In a pan over high heat, cook the onions, garlic, jalapeño, and bell pepper in a couple of tablespoons of water until soft. Add the cooked lentils, taco seasoning, and refried beans and mix well. Add the broth and bring mixture to a boil. Reduce to a simmer, cover, and cook for 5 to 7 minutes, until the lentil-bean mixture is about the thickness of hummus.

Have guests spoon the lentil-bean taco filling into the warm tortillas, then garnish with toppings and salsas of choice.

BURSTING NORI BURRITOS

We are huge fans of nori rolls. It's a blast to roll nori with family and friends at home, or at the fire-house. Our newest invention is to mix the sticky short-grain brown rice with black quinoa! There's at least a dozen different ways to load up your roll depending on what veggies you like. Below are some of our favorite vegetables, but most of all we want to encourage you to roll your own nori. And customize all you want—I like my nori dipped in Lightning Dressing (page 91).

Makes 4 rolls

1 cup cooked short-grain brown rice

1 cup cooked black quinoa

Brown rice vinegar, if needed

4 sheets toasted nori

1 cucumber, peeled and cut into long strips

2 beets, cooked and cut into strips

1 avocado, cut into strips

½ cup carrots, shredded

½ cup sliced green onions

½ cup broccoli sprouts

4 to 6 bok choy, cut into strips

2 cups fresh spinach leaves

A few leaves Boston lettuce

½ red or orange bell pepper, cut into strips

1 mango, peeled, pitted, and cut into strips

Wasabi powder, mixed with water to make a paste

Pickled ginger

Low-sodium tamari

Place the cooked rice and quinoa in a large bowl and stir together until they become sort of sticky—to the point where the mixture holds onto the spoon. (If the rice is not sticking to the quinoa, stir in a few drops of brown rice vinegar until the grains become sticky.)

Place 1 sheet of nori flat on a dry surface. Spread about ¾ cup quinoa and rice mixture on three-fourths of the flat sheet, leaving the top fourth of the sheet bare. Place your choice of cucumber, beet, avocado, carrots, green onions, sprouts, bok choy, spinach, lettuce, bell peppers, and mango (or vegetables of your choice) horizontally across the middle of the flattened quinoa and rice.

(If you plan to eat this like a huge hand-held burrito, and if you feel daring, add a layer of wasabi paste and pickled ginger alongside the other vegetables—it would be difficult to add ginger and wasabi with both hands holding tight!)

Using both hands, starting from the quinoa-rice end, roll up the sheet and fillings. It may be rough going at first, but just keep rolling and rolling until the end you started with connects to the bare end. The ends will stick together easily if the quinoa and rice are still a little warm. If the ends of the nori do not stick, try dabbing the edge of the bare end with water or a juicy bit of mango. Repeat to make 4 rolls.

You can slice the rolls into ½-inch, medallion-style pieces. If you do so, make sure you use a sharp knife and hold the roll together while you slice.

Serve the nori pieces with dishes of pickled ginger, wasabi paste, and tamari, dipping the nori itself, or each piece of sliced nori, into one or all of the toppings.

OATMEAL-RAISIN
CHOCOLATE CHIP COOKIES
(page 263)

CHAPTER 9

DESSERTS

HOT SHOT BISCOTTI

Hot Shots are the firefighters who are dropped into the path of a forest fire to try to stem its destruction. These biscotti are loaded with flavor, crunch, and enough calories to keep hunger away as you problem-solve the forest fires raging in your life. Grab a Hot Shot Biscot (sounds cool shortened like that, no?) and you are ready to trot!

Makes 16 to 20 biscotti

⅔ **cup walnuts**

2 tablespoons water

½ **cup 100% pure maple syrup**

1 tablespoon vanilla extract

1 cup white whole wheat flour

½ **cup oat flour**

¼ **cup old-fashioned oats**

⅓ **cup dried cranberries**

⅓ **cup raw hazelnuts, toasted in a 350°F oven for 5 to 8 minutes or until fragrant**

⅓ **cup pistachios**

⅓ **cup nondairy chocolate chips and/or raisins**

Preheat the oven to 350°F. Line a baking sheet with parchment paper.

In a food processor, blend the walnuts and water until the mixture becomes a lump. Add the maple syrup and vanilla and blend until uniformly mixed. Pulse in the flours and oats with as few rotations of the blade as possible; this keeps the flour from toughening up. Add the cranberries, hazelnuts, pistachios, and chocolate chips and/or raisins and blend a few times more.

Remove the biscotti dough from the processor and form into a roughly 9x3-inch log. Place on the lined pan and bake for 25 minutes. Set aside to cool. Decrease the oven temperature to 300°F.

When the biscotti log is cool enough to handle (5 to 8 minutes), use a serrated knife to slice into ½-inch slices. Place the slices flat on the same lined baking pan. Bake for 10 minutes, flip, and bake again for 10 more minutes, until both sides are lightly browned. Cool and serve when crisp!

STONES SCONES

When Jane first started making these her kids thought she was saying *stones,* not *scones.* They provide a mountain of calories for those who exercise more than two hours a day and are looking for plant-based ways of keeping caloric intake up there!

TIP: Sometimes we use a glass or cookie cutter to make round shapes, which are smaller than the wedges. Or if we're in a real hurry, we use a spoon and simply scoop out about 10 scones: These tops bake with a jagged texture and brown nicely, thus truly earning the name *stones.* Both kinds of the smaller scones bake for only 15 minutes, until lightly browned.

Makes 8 scones

1½ cups oat flour

1½ cups almond flour (also called almond meal)

½ cup 100% pure maple syrup

1 tablespoon vanilla extract

1 tablespoon water

⅓ cup add-ins like a mix of dried fruit, pistachios, walnuts, or nondairy chocolate chips

---

Preheat the oven to 400°F. Line a baking sheet with parchment paper.

In a bowl, combine the flours. Add the maple syrup, vanilla, and water and gently fold the ingredients together with a rubber spatula until the dough forms into a solid clump. Fold in the dried fruit, nuts, or chocolate chips.

On the lined pan, press out the dough to a round that is an inch-plus thick; wet your fingers a bit to help keep the dough from sticking. Use a pizza cutter or a sharp knife to cut the dough into 8 wedges. Arrange the wedges about ¼ inch apart on the baking sheet.

Bake for 18 minutes, until browned on top. Keep an eye on them as they brown up quickly. If possible, serve warm.

SEED BARK PUCKS

These pucks, using the same ingredients as our granola on page 35, pack a crispy crunch and leave people asking, "Wait, that was really good—what's in there?" No worries. It is all good.

Use a glass to create cookie or puck shapes; that way all the extra seed bark in between the pucks becomes a great crumbly topping for your bowl of oatmeal. The pucks are the perfect snappy little snack bite, or foundation for the dinner-party dessert, Raspberry Pudding Crumble Parfait, on page 253.

Makes 12 to 16 pucks

1½ cups raw pumpkin seeds

½ cup raw sunflower seeds

¼ cup raw sesame seeds

¼ cup flaxseed meal

2 tablespoons chia seeds

2 to 3 tablespoons 100% pure maple syrup (just enough to barely coat the blended ingredients)

Preheat the oven to 350°F. Line a baking sheet with parchment paper.

In a bowl, combine the pumpkin seeds, sunflower seeds, sesame seeds, flaxseed meal, chia seeds, and maple syrup. Toss all the ingredients until well coated. Place the mixture onto the lined pan and press out to a ¼- to ⅓-inch thickness.

Use a glass or a cookie cutter to create puck shapes throughout the mixture. Bake for 18 minutes, or until fragrant and lightly browned on top. Rotate the pan halfway through if your oven bakes unevenly. Do not let them burn.

Remove from the oven and let the pucks cool; you can hear them crackling as they cool. This is an important stage as this is when the granola stiffens and gets crispy. After cooling for 20 to 30 minutes you can pick up the pucks and snack on all the crispy bits in between.

HOUSE ARREST CREAMY CHOCOLATE PUDDING

Our aunt called to say she was under house arrest for an expired driver's license, and wanted our chocolate pudding recipe. After making it, she said until she gets a new license she is going to stay at home eating House Arrest Creamy Chocolate Pudding. It is so creamy and dreamy you, too, won't mind being under house arrest!

Serves 4

1 (12-ounce) package firm, silken, "lite" tofu (yes it has to fit those 3 descriptors or it will not work. We suggest Mori-Nu brand)

3 tablespoons cocoa powder

4 to 5 tablespoons 100% pure maple syrup, as sweetness preferences vary

½ teaspoon vanilla extract

Wrap the block of tofu in a cloth napkin, then another napkin and another. There should be 3 to 5 layers of absorbent cloth surrounding the tofu. Apply a bit of pressure to the block—it is OK if the block breaks into larger sections. After draining for 3 hours (or overnight in the fridge), the tofu is ready to use. (When you're under house arrest, you have plenty of time to drain your tofu!)

In a food processor or high-speed blender, combine the tofu, cocoa, maple syrup, and vanilla. Blend until there are no visible small flecks of tofu. It will be a thick creamy consistency ready to eat or spread as frosting.

RASPBERRY PUDDING

The raspberries in this pudding make it a beautiful bright pink. *This recipe only works if the correct tofu is used: It must be firm, silken, and "lite."* (We like Mori-Nu, available online, if not locally.) Otherwise the results can be runny like a milkshake or rough like cat litter. Yikes, be sure to find the correct type of tofu!

Serves 8 (if you don't taste-test too much of it)

2 (12-ounce) packages firm, silken, "lite" tofu

1 cup frozen raspberries

½ to ¾ cup 100% pure maple syrup

2 tablespoons lemon juice, or more to taste

The night before if possible, wrap the tofu cubes in 4 to 6 cloth napkins. The cloth soaks the moisture out of the tofu, which will help the pudding be thicker in texture. If you don't get to this the night before, don't worry: Any amount of time wrapped in cloth napkins will help—even a few minutes.

Once the tofu has been drained, combine the tofu, raspberries, maple syrup, and lemon juice in a food processor. Blend until smooth. Serve immediately or store in the refrigerator in an airtight container until ready to be gobbled up.

RASPBERRY PUDDING CRUMBLE PARFAIT

This is a colorful dessert with a crispy twist. You will win over kids after school with this layered snack, or wow your dinner party when you serve in wine glasses.

Serves 8

Raspberry Pudding (page 251)
Seed Bark Granola (page 35) or Seed Bark Pucks (page 248)
1 cup fresh raspberries (optional)

Spoon half of the pudding into 8 dessert cups or small bowls (or wine glasses for an extra touch of elegance). Sprinkle with half the granola, or place pucks on top. Top with the remaining pudding for another layer, and finally the remaining granola or pucks. Add a cluster of raspberries on top if you like and serve.

BADASS BANANA BREAD

We love it when we have brown bananas around because it means Badass Banana Bread. You will *oooh* and *ahhh* over the way your house smells while it's baking. In fact, if you are having repairs made to your house, make the bread for the workers and see if you can get 20 percent off your bill—just like we did! Now that's badass. (See photo, page 105.)

Depending on what pan you have you can make banana bread, muffins, or donuts.

Makes 1 loaf, 12 muffins, or 12 donuts

2 cups whole-grain flour (we use 1 cup whole wheat flour and 1 cup oat flour)

1 teaspoon baking powder

½ teaspoon baking soda

1 teaspoon cinnamon

¼ teaspoon nutmeg

3 brown-spotted medium bananas, peeled and smashed (1¼ to 1½ cups)

¼ cup 100% pure maple syrup

¼ cup water

2 tablespoons unsweetened applesauce

1 tablespoon vanilla extract

1 teaspoon apple cider vinegar

⅓ cup add-ins of your choice: walnuts, pistachios, raisins, or nondairy chocolate chips (I have sort of a heavy hand here and probably use more like ½ cup to make it even more badass)

Preheat the oven to 400°F. Line a loaf pan with parchment paper (or get out a nonstick muffin pan or nonstick donut pan).

In a bowl, combine the flour, baking powder, baking soda, cinnamon, and nutmeg. In a large bowl, combine the bananas, maple syrup, water, applesauce, vanilla, and vinegar. Mix the dry ingredients into the wet. Fold in the add-ins.

Pour the batter into the lined loaf pan (or divide among 12 muffin or donut cups). Bake the loaf for 30 minutes (or the muffins or donuts for 15 to 18 minutes), until golden brown on top. Serve warm!

LABOR DAY ZUCCHINI BREAD

Labor Day is the time of the year that gardens everywhere unleash their zucchinis. We shred ours up and make loaf after loaf of zucchini bread for our Labor Day family reunion. (See photo, page 105.)

Like the banana bread on page 254, you can make zucchini bread, muffins, or donuts.

Makes 1 loaf, 12 muffins, or 12 donuts

2 cups whole-grain flour (we use 1 cup whole wheat flour and 1 cup oat flour)

1 teaspoon baking powder

½ teaspoon baking soda

½ teaspoon cinnamon

1¾ cups shredded zucchini, lightly squeezed in a dish towel to remove some of the water

⅔ cup 100% pure maple syrup

1 teaspoon vanilla extract

Preheat the oven to 400°F. Line a loaf pan with parchment paper (or get out a nonstick muffin pan or nonstick donut pan).

In a bowl, combine the flour, baking powder, baking soda, and cinnamon. In a large bowl, combine the zucchini, maple syrup, and vanilla and stir. Mix the dry ingredients into the wet.

Pour the batter into the lined loaf pan (or divide among 12 muffin or donut cups). Bake the loaf for 30 minutes (or the muffins or donuts for 15 to 18 minutes), until golden brown on top. Serve warm.

BEAR SCAT

You will love these treats right out of the freezer! They are *growling* good! This aptly named, frozen dessert is guaranteed to entertain your guests as they bite into the cool and refreshing chocolate-covered blueberries. We would like to thank plant-based Karen from Temagami, Ontario, Canada, who has seen her fair share of bears and bear scat, for this decadent, hilariously named treat!

Makes 10 to 12 pieces

1 cup nondairy chocolate chips
1 cup fresh blueberries

Line a baking sheet with parchment paper.

In a double boiler or in the microwave melt the chocolate chips. (*A tip for microwave users:* Melt the chocolate in multiple, short increments, stirring in between. This avoids burning, which can happen quickly. Three 30-second increments (90 seconds total) with stirring in between seems about perfect.)

Once the chocolate is melted, add the blueberries and stir. Place tablespoon-size scoops of the mixture on the lined pan. Place the pan in the freezer for at least 1 hour—overnight works best!

I am very lucky to have found Engine 2 when I needed it most. In Summer 2015 I was in pretty good health (so I thought). But I started feeling tightness in my throat whenever I tried to exercise. Thinking it was acid reflux, I pushed it off until my wife had a hunch and insisted I see a cardiologist. Turns out, I had a 99% blockage in my right coronary artery. At 41, I was a heart disease patient! My wife had introduced me to a whole food, plant-based diet previously but I mostly ignored her pleas—until that day. I knew that Engine 2 had a ton of recipes and foods that were "man-friendly," so I immediately bought all of Rip's books. The food was so good, it made going plant-strong easy! Plant-strong meat-loaf, pasta and pizza became my favorite meals, and as my cholesterol and weight fell, I realized I didn't miss the foods I used to eat at all. Really it was the opposite—those foods nearly killed me! I truly feel like I understand what "plant-strong" means now. I am fueling my body and making it stronger every day—thanks to Engine 2!

—TODD MITCHELL, BUFFALO, NEW YORK

FROZEN FROSTED FUDGE SQUARES

The inspiration for these came from *The Happy Pear*—a beautiful cookbook written by David and Stephen Flynn, identical twins from Ireland! "These can't be vegan" was the first comment (compliment!) Jane heard about the brownies from her son who does not have a sweet tooth. Jane and her daughters finished the pan, no problem!

Makes 12 brownie squares

1 ¼ cups walnuts

¼ cup water

1 cup 100% pure maple syrup

¾ cup cocoa powder

1 teaspoon vanilla extract

1 ¼ cups cooked peeled sweet potato (about 1 medium sweet potato)

½ cup oat flour

¼ cup shelled pistachios, coarsely chopped

In a food processor, blend the walnuts and water until they form a clump. Add the maple syrup, cocoa powder, and vanilla and blend until smooth, about 2 minutes. Scoop half of the chocolate mixture into a small bowl and set aside for the frosting.

Cook the sweet potato in whatever way works best for you until soft throughout: Bake in a 400°F oven for 45 minutes, or cook in the microwave for 8 minutes. Peel the sweet potato.

To the chocolate mixture still in the food processor add the cooked sweet potato and blend until smooth, about a minute. To the mixture add the oat flour and gently pulse until the flour is incorporated.

Sprinkle half of the chopped pistachios on the bottom of a 9x9-inch baking pan. Add the brownie mix from the processor, spread it out, then top with the reserved frosting. Sprinkle the rest of the pistachios on top of the frosting. Cover and freeze for at least an hour before serving. Thaw for a few minutes before serving as it makes it easier to cut into squares.

PUMPKIN POUND CAKE

This recipe is super moist—so moist that our neighbors dubbed it Pumpkin Pound Cake due to the weight of just carrying it across the street.

Makes 1 loaf

---

1 ¼ cups pumpkin purée

½ cup 100% pure maple syrup

1 teaspoon vanilla extract

¼ cup water

1 cup white whole wheat flour (we prefer King Arthur brand)

1 cup oat flour

1 teaspoon baking powder

½ teaspoon baking soda

1 teaspoon ground cinnamon

1 to 1½ teaspoons pumpkin pie spice, your preference for pumpkin flavor

¼ cup dried currants, cranberries, raisins, or nondairy chocolate chips (optional)

Preheat the oven to 400°F. Line a loaf pan with parchment paper.

In a large mixing bowl, combine the pumpkin, maple syrup, vanilla, and water and stir. In another bowl, combine the flours, baking powder, baking soda, cinnamon, and pumpkin pie spice and stir well. Add the dry ingredients to the wet and mix until all ingredients are well combined. Add the currants if using, and stir again.

Pour the batter into the lined loaf pan. Bake for 40 minutes, until the middle of the cake is springy and not moist to the touch. Serve warm as is, or with Banana Butter (page 104).

OATMEAL-RAISIN CHOCOLATE CHIP COOKIES

This dough can be made into balls or smashed flat. Our mom insists that cookies should be flat and crisp, while we prefer them round and softer inside. In our oven, the pan looks like an elephant stepped on part of it—half the cookies are flat and half are round balls. Either way, the recipe makes 12 great cookies.

Makes 12 cookies

¾ cup oat flour

¼ cup old-fashioned oats

¼ cup 100% pure maple syrup

¼ cup almond butter or peanut butter

1 tablespoon flaxseed meal

1½ teaspoons vanilla extract

¼ cup raisins

¼ cup nondairy dark chocolate chips

Preheat the oven to 350°F. Line a baking sheet with parchment paper.

In a bowl, stir together all the ingredients. When the ingredients are well combined, portion the dough on the lined pan in roughly 1-tablespoon scoops. Leave them round or press them flat—your choice.

Bake for 12 to 15 minutes, until lightly browned. Try not to eat them all at once!

YONANAS SOFT SERVE

Firefighters love their ice cream. Here is an alternative that will amaze your firehouse or family. It transforms frozen bananas by sending them through a Yonanas dessert maker or other ice cream machine. It comes out just like soft-serve ice cream from Dairy Queen but without the moo factor. We are amazed each time we make it! Our favorite flavors are banana with frozen mango and/or frozen raspberries. A frozen banana is the base and the other frozen fruit changes the color and flavor to your Yonanas. This recipe makes 4 servings (about 2 servings per banana), but it's easy to scale the recipe up or down, depending on your preference.

Serves 4

2 ripe bananas, peeled and frozen

1 cup frozen fruit of your choice: mangoes, blueberries, raspberries, blackberries

If using a Yonanas dessert maker, the bananas may be frozen whole. Other machines may require the bananas to be sliced into sections before freezing. Process the bananas and fruit in an ice cream maker according to the manufacturer's directions and be amazed at what you have created.

To serve, sprinkle with chocolate balsamic vinegar, a little pure vanilla extract, nutmeg, and/or a sprinkle of Grape-Nuts cereal for crunch.

I am only thirty-eight years old. I do not have high blood pressure, cholesterol, or heart disease. I have been a "vegan" since I was sixteen years old as I truly never liked the taste of meat and I was allergic to dairy.

Soon after my seventeenth birthday, my forty-seven-year-old mother passed away suddenly from a massive heart attack. She had lived a life with high blood pressure, which I believed at the time was managed by pills. I remember that she came home from work early to take me to my basketball game but instead, asked that my brother take me. She said she wasn't feeling well but that she would be there later. She asked if I could get her a soda so that she could burp to relieve the pressure in her chest. She thought she had indigestion.

That was the last time I ever saw her. She died alone in our house while the paramedics raced over to help her. Incidentally, I had the highest scoring game of my high school career that night. I truly believe she was true to her word and was at my game.

Raised by a working father and a brother who did not handle the death of my mother very well, I was left on my own without any female influence in my life.

Fast forward a few years and I have two gorgeous little girls ages seven and four. I refuse to leave this world, especially if the power is in my own hands.

I wish I knew at seventeen what I know now because my mom might still be here. My father is seventy-one and has had one heart attack, a partial blockage and has three stents. He struggles trying to follow this plan on his own and is often stubborn in his ways and has a doubting spouse who believes in moderation. I feel hopeless living 3,000 miles away.

What I can focus on now is the future of my family. I want my children to have a fighting chance in this world and I want them to have two parents who can not only babysit the grandkids someday but also run and play with them as well.

I just wanted to let you all know that you are touching and affecting younger generations too who are passing this way of living on to their kids.

Thank you, from the bottom of my plant-strong heart.

—PAM KROPF AND FAMILY: CHARLIE, 42; SIERRA, 7; AND JACQUELINE, 4

ACKNOWLEDGMENTS

We would like to jump up and offer a big high five to everyone who helped with this book. Whether it was through time in your kitchen or our kitchen, proofreading or taste-testing, sharing a recipe or sharing your opinion, your inspiration and influence has helped create this book.

We are over the moon appreciative of Grand Central Publishing and Jamie Raab, Matthew Ballast, Nick Small, Katherine Stopa, Sheila Oakes, Karen Murgolo, Tareth Mitch, and our spectacular editor, Sarah Pelz. Thank you for pumping out another Engine 2 book with rib-sticking recipes!

Special thanks to Ann Esselstyn, Essy Esselstyn, Char Nolan, Ami Mackey, Laurie Kortowich, Brenda Reed, Paula Stiechen, Sandy Spallino, Jillian Gibson, Stephanie Sullivan, Pennie Rand, Elizabeth Keene, Cindy Pierce, Kristin Brown, Karen Currier, Elaine Jutras, John Fitzgerald, Theresa Cary, Lori Palmer, Brenda Fahrenkopf, Toni Kulma, Selena Kimble, Cheryl Forror, Erica Cambarare, Lisa Hamilton, Darlene Kelbach, Erin Vesey, Nate Turner, Dani Little, Jay and Adele Stint, Ricky and Susie Taft, Renee Deman, Jackie Acho, Brian Hart, Ted Esselstyn, Anne Bingham, Zeb Esselstyn, Polly LaBarre, Jill Kolasinski, Bryan and Heather Kolasinski, Jeff Novick, Adam Sud, Susie Crile, Tim and Nicole DeBoom, David and Stephen Flynn (*The Happy Pear*), Rouxbe, Hugh Tobin of Yonanas, and Plant-Based CLE.

A big shout out to our literary agent Richard Pine for continuing to do what he does best.

We want to thank Jane's Labrador retriever, Fraser, for his patience during all the recipe testing and during the recipe photography.

And lastly, we want to flood Donna Turner Ruhlman with thanks for her photography. She is the reason our food looks so smoking hot!

INDEX

ABOUT THE AUTHORS

RIP ESSELSTYN was born in upstate New York, raised in Cleveland, Ohio, and attended the University of Texas at Austin, where he was a three-time All-American swimmer and majored in speech communications. After graduation Rip spent a decade as one of the premier triathletes in the world. He then joined the Austin Fire Department where he introduced his passion for a plant-strong lifestyle to Austin's Engine 2 Firehouse in order to rescue a firefighting brother's health. To document his success, he wrote the national bestselling book, *The Engine 2 Diet,* which shows the irrefutable connection between a plant-based diet and good

health. His second book, *Plant-Strong,* became a #1 *New York Times* bestseller. And his third book, *The Engine 2 Seven-Day Rescue Diet,* sparked a plant-strong awakening in homes everywhere!

Nine years ago, Rip left his job as a firefighter to team up with Whole Foods Market as one of their Healthy Eating Partners to raise the awareness of team members, customers, and communities about the benefits of eating a whole-food, plant-strong diet. He has appeared on numerous national television shows, including *Today, CBS This Morning, Good Morning America,* and *The Dr. Oz Show.*

Rip is married to Jill Kolasinski and they have three children: Kole, Sophie, and Hope. They live in Austin, Texas.

JANE ESSELSTYN graduated from the University of Michigan, where she competed nationally as a recruited swimmer and rower. She is an avid and inventive designer of plant-strong recipes and the co-author of *The Prevent and Reverse Heart Disease Cookbook.* She created the recipe sections of the #1 *New York Times*–bestseller *Plant-Strong,* as well as *The Engine 2 Seven-Day Rescue Diet,* both by Rip Esselstyn. Jane is a fresh, charismatic voice, bringing her perspective and passion as a nurse, researcher, mother, and teacher to her presentations, food demonstrations, and cookbooks with clarity, hilarity, and a can-do attitude.

Jane and her husband, Brian Hart, live in Cleveland, Ohio, with their three children—Crile, Zeb and Bainon—and enjoy a plant-based diet.

3 1333 04648 0008